RYA
GO GREEN!

A young person's guide to
the blue planet

Where there's water, there's life

RYA Go Green!

Words and Illustrations by: Claudia Myatt
Technical Editor: Dr Susie Tomson
Foreword by: Ben Ainslie C.B.E.

© Claudia Myatt 2010
First Published RYA 2010

The Royal Yachting Association
RYA House
Ensign Way
Hamble
Southampton
SO31 4YA

Tel: 0845 345 0400
Fax: 0845 345 0329
E-mail: publications@rya.org.uk
Web: www.rya.org.uk

ISBN: 978-1906435011
RYA Order Code: G75

Totally Chlorine Free   **Sustainable Forests**

Cover Design: Claudia Myatt
Typeset: Creativebyte
Proofreading and indexing: Alan Thatcher
Printed in China through: World Print

FOREWORD
by Ben Ainslie C.B.E.

Sailing has become not only my passion but my life, and most of my time is spent on or around water. There's more to winning races than just handling the boat; interacting with wind, waves and tides so intensively makes me very aware of the special and fragile nature of the marine environment. RYA Go Green! is an excellent way to explore and appreciate all aspects of the wet stuff that is not only our playground but our life.

We all have a responsibility for our actions and for yachtsmen it is no different. The RYA's fantastic Green Blue programme has provided practical solutions for many day to day environmental issues facing the sea. I have been working with others looking at ways we can reduce our environmental footprint. I am an optimist and believe that with the right information we can all make the right decisions.

RYA Go Green! increases our understanding of the amazing world of water so we can make informed choices and leave rivers, estuaries and oceans that we are proud to pass on to the next generation.

We can all take small steps to reduce our impact—it's not just sailors like me who depend upon the sea! For me, understanding and looking after the environment is just another aspect of improving performance.

CONTENTS

Foreword by Ben Ainslie CBE

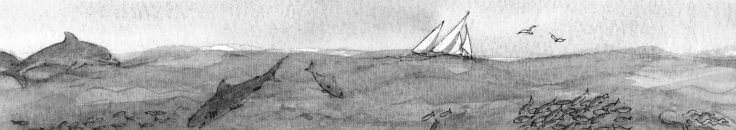

The story of the oceans begins in outer space and finishes inside your body.   Take a journey with Albert Ross and friends to find out how water connects us all...

ALBERT ROSS

TINA TERN

MOBY DUCK

CHLOE CRAB

PLANET OCEAN

Even if you've never been on the sea, or only get to wriggle your toes in a rockpool once a year, you depend on water in more ways than you could ever dream of.

So come with me to find out how the oceans began and exactly what they do for us.

Albert Ross

Nearly three quarters of the world's surface is covered in water — but it wasn't always like that. Let's go right back to the beginning, to a time more than four billion years ago...

The earth *began* as a hot, waterless lump of rock, volcanoes and minerals. Because it had no atmosphere, it was bombarded by lumps of rock from space which covered it in a cloud of dust and gas.

Mmm... we'll give that one a miss

Nobody lived there... well, who'd want to!

It took a few million years for the earth to cool down. As it cooled, some of the gases condensed into such heavy clouds that eventually it started to rain... and rain and rain... for thousands of years.

As the water filled up all the shallow parts and minerals were washed out of the rocks, turning the water salty.

The first oceans were soupy, gloopy and steamy. You wouldn't want to swim in them but, they were full of the right kind of stuff for really basic life forms to develop... and then gradually more complex creatures evolved.

Come on in, the water's lovely!

Eventually some animals got smart enough to get out of the oceans altogether. But all forms of life — even aliens — need water to survive, and this is the only planet we know of that's got plenty!

How many millions make a billion? In Europe, it used to be a million million, but these days the American version, a thousand million, is in general use. So 4 billion years looks like this — 4,000,000,000.

If that makes your head hurt, just think of it as a very, very, very long time ago!

Once the rain had stopped and the oceans had filled up, you still wouldn't have recognised Planet Earth as it looked completely different. Even the continents have moved around!

GIANT JIGSAW PIECES

225 million years ago the land was all clumped together and surrounded by one enormous ocean. But the land isn't fixed — it's like bits of toast floating on a bowl of thick molten rock soup.

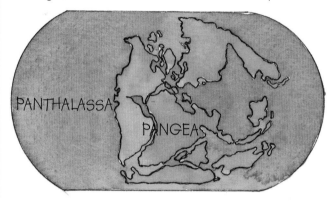

Can you make out the shapes of today's continents in this giant jigsaw puzzle?

UNZIP THE ATLANTIC...

By about 80 million years ago the crusts of land had split up and drifted apart. Over millions of years they formed the continents that we know today.

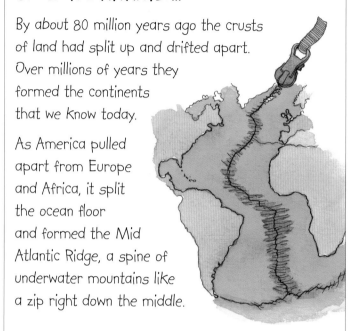

As America pulled apart from Europe and Africa, it split the ocean floor and formed the Mid Atlantic Ridge, a spine of underwater mountains like a zip right down the middle.

FAST MOVER!

In 1963 a fishing boat off the coast of Iceland noticed smoke rising from the sea, thought it must be a ship on fire, and went over to have a look. But it wasn't a boat — it was an underwater volcano throwing cloud, ash and steam out of the water. As the volcano kept erupting, it broke the surface and an island began to form, spewing out lava and ash faster than the sea could wash it away.

By 1965 the volcano had calmed down, but the island remains, and is still studied carefully by scientists to see what happens to new land. Birds, insects and vegetation have all appeared, and human interference is kept to a minimum to see how the island develops naturally.

What do you mean, it wasn't here last time?

ROCK SOLID?

It may feel like the ground beneath your feet is rock solid, but the continents are still floating around on top of the earth's core.

But don't panic, the movement is very, very, very slow. Planets work on a much slower timescale to humans! In planet years, human history has happened faster than the blink of an eye.

Don't be silly, America can't have moved!

How fast do continents move? America and Europe are still drifting apart at the rate of 2cm each year!

UNDER THE SURFACE

The ocean floor is not just a level plain where nothing happens except a few fish swimming around. There are undersea volcanoes, hot steam vents, earthquakes, deep trenches and mountains so big they make Mount Everest look like a small hill.

Only a small part of the ocean floor has been explored. We know more about the surface of the moon than we do about the ocean floor!

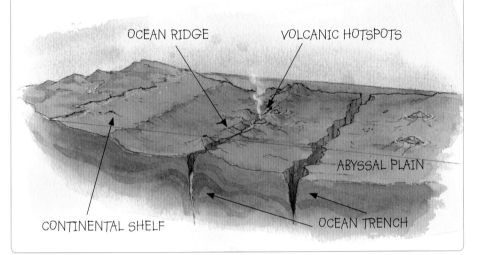

OCEAN RIDGE   VOLCANIC HOTSPOTS

ABYSSAL PLAIN

CONTINENTAL SHELF   OCEAN TRENCH

The deepest parts of the oceans are home for some of the strangest creatures on the planet, beyond your wildest imagination. They can survive in the dark, under huge water pressure, around scalding hot underwater vents, or so far down that they produce their own light to see each other.

POMPEII WORM

I'm cool!

Address: Around scalding hot underwater vents that spurt out jets of superheated water and steam.

Favourite meal: sulphur-eating bacteria. Yummy!

TWINKLE TWINKLE, LITTLE SQUID...

What do you do if you live in a place the sun can never reach? Make your own light! Many deepwater creatures have bioluminescence so they can find each other in the dark, attract food or confuse other creatures.

ANGLER FISH

Address: Anywhere deep and dark

Favourite meal: anything! Food is rare in my part of the ocean, so I have a built-in fishing line and luminous lure dangling from my head. Works every time.

I'm gorgeous!

DEEP DOWN AND DARK...

The deepest part of the ocean is thought to be the Mariana Trench in the western Pacific. It's almost 11,000 metres deep — that's about seven miles! It's formed where one of the plates on the earth's crust dives down under another.

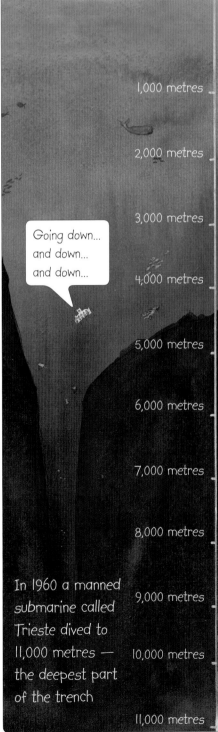

Going down... and down... and down...

1,000 metres

2,000 metres

3,000 metres

4,000 metres

5,000 metres

6,000 metres

7,000 metres

8,000 metres

9,000 metres

In 1960 a manned submarine called Trieste dived to 11,000 metres — the deepest part of the trench

10,000 metres

11,000 metres

OCEAN CURRENTS

We don't just need water to live, we need water that's on the move. Luckily for us, the oceans don't just sit there like a large bath; if they did, the water would stagnate and we'd all be dead. Big ocean currents, called GYRES, flow like giant rivers round the world...

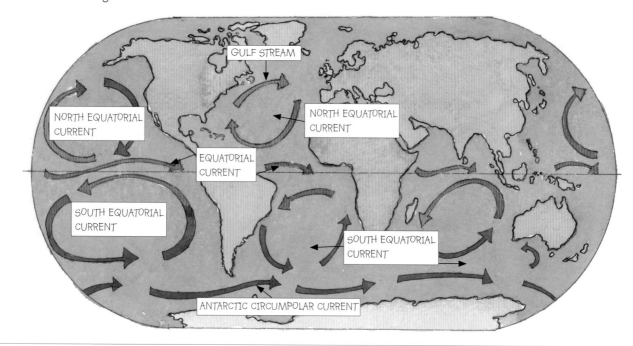

GULF STREAM

NORTH EQUATORIAL CURRENT

NORTH EQUATORIAL CURRENT

EQUATORIAL CURRENT

SOUTH EQUATORIAL CURRENT

SOUTH EQUATORIAL CURRENT

ANTARCTIC CIRCUMPOLAR CURRENT

BATHTIME TALES...

In 1992, during a storm in the Pacific Ocean a container fell off a cargo ship carrying toys to Europe, spilling 46,000 plastic ducks into the sea. For almost twenty years the ducks drifted around the oceans, carried by wind and currents and getting washed up on beaches all over the world. Some became locked in ice in the Arctic, others were washed up on tropical beaches.

The fleet of little yellow ducks has given scientists more information than they have ever had before about how ocean gyres work!

Somehow I wasn't expecting a bath to be this big...

MORE BATHTIME TALES

The spinning of the earth makes the water flow in big circles rather than in a straight line. This is called the Coriolis effect and it makes the water flow clockwise in the Northern Hemisphere, anticlockwise in the Southern Hemisphere.

If you've heard the rumour that water goes down the plughole in a different direction in the North or South Hemisphere, try it where you live. Can you prove the theory right or wrong?

This massive ocean conveyor belt helps to balance the world's climate and weather. A change in climate will affect the oceans — and a change in the oceans will affect the weather...

EL NINO (THE BOY in Spanish)

A sudden change in one ocean current has an effect all over the world. Off the coast of Peru the warm surface water is usually blown westwards across the Pacific, drawing nutrient rich water up to the surface. Occasionally — and no-one is quite sure why — this doesn't happen. The warm water stays close to shore, plankton die off, the fish have nothing to eat, and the fishermen of Peru have nothing to catch. They call this El Nino, and the effects are not just local.

The heat from the static water spreads northward, causing America to experience more tornadoes than usual. At the same time the eastern side of the Pacific gets more drought. It even affects us here in Britain, as our weather systems travel across the Atlantic from America, bringing us more stormy wet summers in an El Nino year. Everything is connected!

GULF STREAM

This *big* river of tropical water gives northern Europe a lovely warm climate compared to our chilly neighbours across the Atlantic in Newfoundland. It was first mapped by American Benjamin Franklin in the 19th century, when he noticed that ships travelling to Europe made much faster times than those coming the other way!

This is what the Gulf Stream would look like if you could *see* the warm water as orange and the cooler water as *blue...*

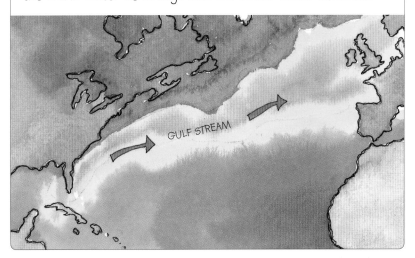

WAVES THAT SWALLOW SHIPS

Another famous ocean current is the Agulhas current which flows down the east coast of Africa. Ships like to catch a ride on this ocean river, as it can give them up to 5 knots extra speed.

But... when the current reaches the bottom of Africa, it meets south westerly winds, strong tides and a sudden drop in the ocean floor, a nasty combination of wind and water power which can kick up enormous, ship swallowing waves.

There's a lot of water on the planet and nearly all of it (97%) is in the sea.

But it doesn't stay there — water is very good at changing its form. It can do liquid (salty or fresh), vapour, and solid (ice).

HYDROLOGIC CYCLE (1)

There's still enough non-salty water around to keep all plants, animals and humans alive thanks to a clever bit of recycling called the hydrologic cycle.

What's a hydrologic cycle? A water powered bicycle, perhaps?

Well, no...

HYDROLOGIC CYCLE (2)

The real hydrologic cycle works something like this...

The amount of water on the planet doesn't change — but it just goes round and round in a continuous cycle of saltwater, vapour, rain and freshwater, occasionally taking turns at being ice.

Sun evaporates surface water from the sea...

Moisture from plants also evaporates from land...

Water vapour gathers as clouds, and falls as rain...

Water soaks into the land and flows back into the sea through rivers and streams

Fresh water doesn't fall evenly all over the planet. The Atacama desert in South America is one of the driest places on earth, with less than 1mm of rain a year. It's so dry that film companies use it when they want to film scenes based on Mars.

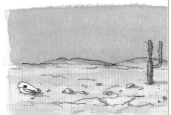

The wettest place on earth are the Khasi Hills in north east India which regularly get up to 12 metres of rain a year. But the people there don't have a problem with floods as the soil is very poor and all the water drains away — so they have a problem with water shortage!

SOLID WATER...

So 3% of the world's water is fresh, not salty — over half of that is locked up in ice. No, not ice cubes, but ice caps at the North and South Poles...

The planet doesn't stay the same temperature, but goes through chilly cycles and warm cycles which have a dramatic effect on all that water. Here's what happens...

THE CHILLY BITS

The polar ice caps are the coldest places on the planet because they get less energy from the sun than the bits round the equator. So when the planet warms up and cools down, it's the polar ice caps that shrink or grow.

During the last ice age, about 18,000 years ago, ice covered about a third of planet's surface, including much of Britain and northern Europe.

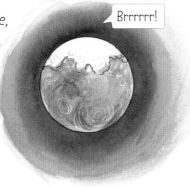

Brrrrrr!

THE BIG FREEZE...

During a big freeze more water is locked up as ice, so sea levels go down all over the world.

During the last ice age you could have walked to France across the English Channel or walked to Russia across the Bering Strait from Alaska.

English Channel — what English Channel?

DOVER YACHT CLUB

THE BIG MELT...

So guess what happens when the planet warms up again and the icecaps shrink? All that water melts back into the sea and sea levels gradually rise.

The earth is still warming up after the last ice age. This should be a gradual process but scientists have noticed it's happening faster than it should. More about global warming in Chapter Seven.

Eeeek!

ICEBERG!

Icebergs form when big lumps of ice break off into the sea from ice sheets and glaciers. The bergs then drift with the currents, breaking up into smaller pieces as they slowly melt. Only about one tenth of the ice shows above the surface.

Scientists keep an eye on big icebergs as they provide valuable information about global warming. In 2008 an iceberg over 100 miles wide broke away from a bigger piece of the Antarctic ice sheet, and its journey is being monitored to see where it goes and how long it lasts. A competition to give the giant iceberg a name was won by six year old Max Dolan, so until it melts to the size of an ice cube, which will probably take about ten years, the berg will be called Melting Bob. Thanks, Max!

Fancy an iceberger?

From the smallest shrimp to the largest whale, the oceans are full of life. Guess which are the most important? Not the biggest — the tiniest! Our lives, and the lives of every creature in the oceans, depend on the smallest life form of all — plankton.

The smallest life forms in the oceans are called plankton. There are two sorts — zooplankton, which are tiny animals, and phytoplankton which are tiny plants.

Like other green plants, phytoplankton absorb carbon dioxide in the atmosphere and swap it for lots of lovely oxygen. This gives us perfect air for breathing and stops the planet getting too hot from too much carbon dioxide. About half our oxygen comes from plankton.

How many? When conditions in the ocean are right, millions of plankton get together and form a bright green patch on the sea that can be seen from space.

FROM BIGGEST TO SMALLEST...

The biggest creature on the planet is the blue whale which grows up to 30 metres long. Its tongue alone weighs as much as an elephant!

The biggest animal in the ocean eats one of the smallest — small shrimps called krill. Because krill are so small, the whale needs to eat an awful lot of them — up to 40 million every day!

Phytoplankton need sunlight, water and minerals to survive. They get the minerals when water circulates, bringing nutrients up from the sea bed.

Each phytoplankton only lives for between one and two days.

How tiny? Under 2mm. So most of them are almost invisible — but there could be at least 100 in a cup of seawater!

What's at the bottom of the sea that provides all this nourishment? Lots of dead fish, dead plankton, more dead fish, dead whales, even more dead fish... All rotting down into a gloopy soup.

Whales make a wide range of noises to communicate and help them navigate through the dark ocean depths. These noises easily carry through the water, and whales can hear each other up to 1,000 miles apart.

The blue whale doesn't have teeth. He takes a large gulp of water and then forces the water out through a comb-like filter in his mouth that the krill can't get through.

The oceans are the *biggest* natural habitat on earth — much of it unexplored by humans. So far over 230,000 different forms of life have been recorded, but scientists know there are thousands more they haven't found yet, especially in the deepest and darkest parts of the ocean.

That's a new one... I'll add it to the list

DINOSAURS OF THE SEA

In 1938 a trawler crew found an odd fish amongst their catch and asked for it to be identified. It turned out to be a coelacanth — a species of fish that has *been* around for over 65 million years. Only fossils of this fish had *ever* been found before, and scientists were amazed to find it alive and well and living in the Indian Ocean.

It would be as astonishing as finding a living dinosaur! Surprisingly, the coelacanth has changed little over the millions of years — it was *obviously* happy the way it was and didn't *see* any need to evolve.

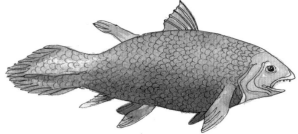

(by the way, it's pronounced 'seal-a-canth' in case you were wondering!)

THE LUNCH BUNCH

All the weird and wonderful creatures in the ocean, from the smallest to the largest, depend upon each other for food. Generally, the smallest creatures get eaten by bigger creatures, which get eaten by bigger ones, which get eaten by even bigger ones. There are a few exceptions like the blue whale, which eats tiny krill.

So, everything depends on the bottom of the food chain — without plankton everything in the ocean would starve!

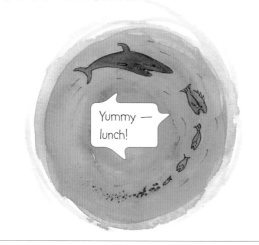

Yummy — lunch!

LIFE IN THE FREEZER

You might think not much can live in the coldest parts of the ocean, but you'd be wrong. The icy waters of Antarctica are oxygen rich and full of tiny shrimp-like creatures called krill which are an important part of the food chain — not just for blue whales but for fish and seabirds too.

Being eaten by anybody nice for lunch today?

It's not just fish and sea mammals who are part of the ocean food chain — thousands of types of seabirds depend on the ocean for their supper too!

OCEAN ADVENTURES

All the oceans are connected — do you know which is which? Sailors used to talk about the 'Seven Seas'

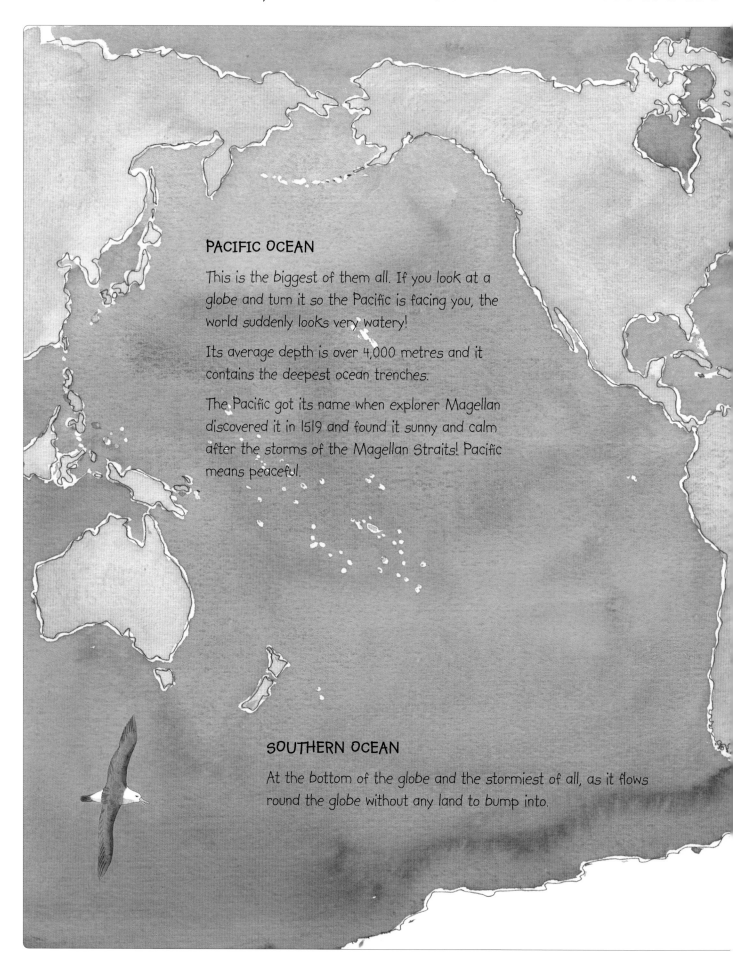

PACIFIC OCEAN

This is the biggest of them all. If you look at a globe and turn it so the Pacific is facing you, the world suddenly looks very watery!

Its average depth is over 4,000 metres and it contains the deepest ocean trenches.

The Pacific got its name when explorer Magellan discovered it in 1519 and found it sunny and calm after the storms of the Magellan Straits! Pacific means peaceful.

SOUTHERN OCEAN

At the bottom of the globe and the stormiest of all, as it flows round the globe without any land to bump into.

... and if you divide both the Pacific and Atlantic into North and South, you have *seven* oceans.

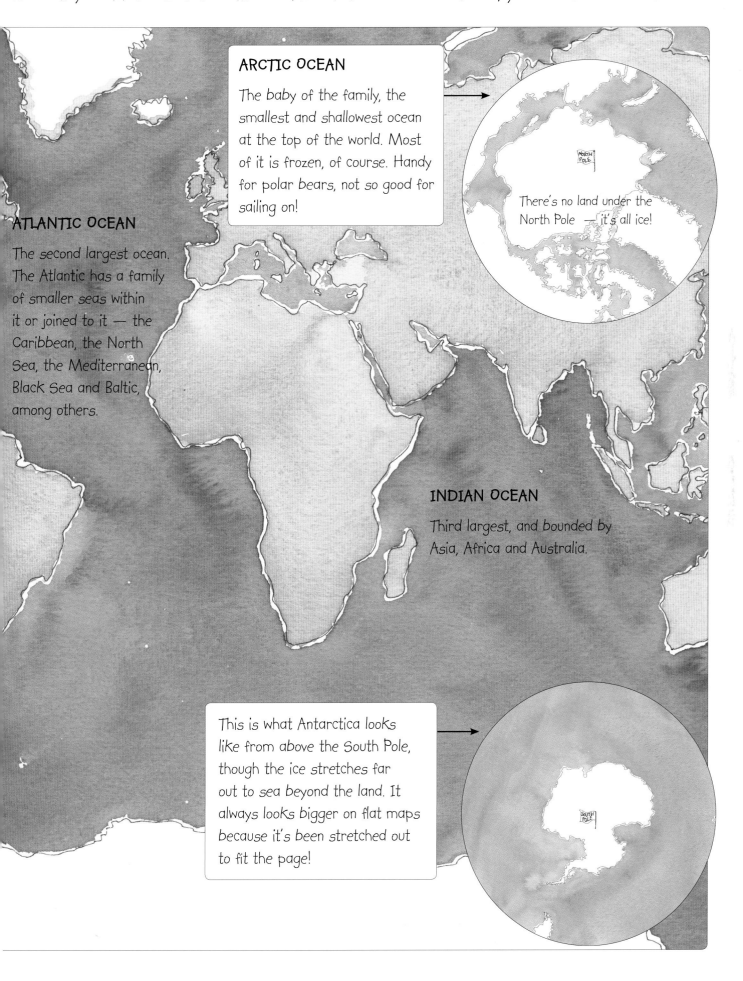

ARCTIC OCEAN

The baby of the family, the smallest and shallowest ocean at the top of the world. Most of it is frozen, of course. Handy for polar bears, not so good for sailing on!

There's no land under the North Pole — it's all ice!

ATLANTIC OCEAN

The second largest ocean. The Atlantic has a family of smaller seas within it or joined to it — the Caribbean, the North Sea, the Mediterranean, Black Sea and Baltic, among others.

INDIAN OCEAN

Third largest, and bounded by Asia, Africa and Australia.

This is what Antarctica looks like from above the South Pole, though the ice stretches far out to sea beyond the land. It always looks bigger on flat maps because it's been stretched out to fit the page!

History is all about the sea. Well at least the interesting bits are — battles, shipwrecks, giant waves and storms; explorers, treasure ships, pirates and taking over new lands...

TRADE WINDS

The spinning of the planet and the movement of hot and cold air keep the winds blowing in a pattern that sailors learnt to rely on. In the days of sail, ships carrying cargo around the world needed the wind behind them to get to where they were going quickly, so the winds were called trade winds.

Ships sailing from Europe to Australia found it easier to keep going east and sail right round the world — even though it meant sailing round stormy Cape Horn on the way home.

> **DID YOU KNOW...**
> The phrase 'being in the doldrums' means being a bit dull and inactive. Sailors used the word doldrums for the area of calms caused by hot air rising at the equator.

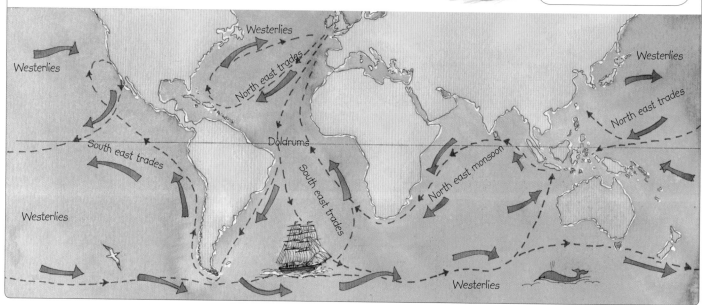

Westerlies

Westerlies

Westerlies

North east trades

Westerlies

South east trades

Doldrums

South east trades

North east monsoon

North east trades

Westerlies

EXPLORING NEW LANDS

Going out of sight of land was a dangerous business when nobody really knew what was out there. Imagine going off into the unknown — with no map!

> I spy with my little eye... something beginning with S...

In the early days of exploration, it was a bit of a miracle if a ship made it home at all.

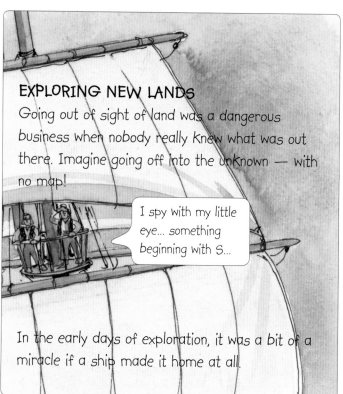

CAPE HORN — the sailor's Everest

Why is Cape Horn so dangerous for boats?

The water of the Southern Ocean narrows in the stormy region between the tip of South America and the continent of Antarctica. Gales blow for over half the year and waves can reach up to 20 metres.

Greetings from Cape Horn
Wish I wasn't here!

BOXES AND MORE BOXES

Next time you buy something from a high street or online shop, think about where it came from. Everything that wasn't made locally has been brought in from another country, probably by ship. Container ships, piled high with metal boxes, carry manufactured goods all around the world. Cranes unload the containers straight onto waiting lorries and trains.

The biggest container ship is 400 metres long and can carry over 10,000 containers. Phew!

OOPS!

Containers are clipped together and lashed down — but they're big and heavy, and every year several thousand fall off into the sea during storms. They float for a while just under the surface, then gradually their cargo spills into the sea. Remember all those plastic ducks? Shoes, laptops, toys, clothes, electronics... all end up on the bottom of the sea or washed up on the beach.

TANKERS

Every country in the world needs oil, but only a few countries produce it. The biggest oil tankers, called Ultra Large Crude Carriers are over 400 metres long and carry millions of litres of oil around the oceans. They only need a small crew to sail them, and can be steered with a small joystick!

Tankers don't hit the rocks very often, but when they do it's a major disaster for everyone, taking years to clean up.

How very crude...

Ports have very strict rules to make sure all ships stay safe and keep off the rocks.

FULL CIRCLE?

As fuel oil becomes more expensive, ship builders are beginning to look again to wind power to help move big ships around the world. But the sailing ships of tomorrow will look very different from square rigged windjammers — they'll have high-tech electronically controlled wing sails, or be pulled along by a very large kite...

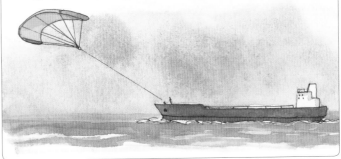

DID YOU KNOW... that sea transport is the most environmentally friendly way to transport goods? More than 90% of trade between countries is transported by sea.

There are no new lands to explore today, but going to sea is still as exciting as ever — and a bit safer than it used to be!

> I wish somebody would hurry up and invent gps...

There are many ways for you poor land bound humans to visit this amazing watery world and understand more about it.

You can do it the hard way on a small yacht or the easy way on a large cruise ship, but you must never forget that you are a guest in my world, and the oceans need care and respect...

CRUISING — THE BIG SHIPS

If you like your ocean travel to be luxurious with plenty of shopping opportunities, a cruise liner is for you (or, if you're short of cash, get a job on board).

The biggest liners carry over 6,000 passengers, but if you don't fancy that much company, there are smaller ones to choose from.

> This wasn't quite what I meant by 'running away to sea'...

Holidaymakers like to cruise to the most beautiful areas of the ocean, but these are also the places most sensitive to pollution. One large cruise ship produces over 50 tons of rubbish each week, so they have to make sure it all gets taken safely back to shore and doesn't mess up the sea.

CHOOSY CRUISING

Many small cruise ships visit some unusual places and give you a chance to see wildlife like whales close up. If you prefer icebergs to ice cream, you can even cruise to Antarctica or Alaska.

> Ice with your drink, sir?

HAUL AWAY HOLIDAYS

The age of sail is still very much with us — choose from a luxury square rigged sailing ship in the Caribbean or learn the ropes on a more workmanlike sailing training ship or charter yacht.

You can go round the world without touching land but you can't go round the world without crossing the sea — unless you're flying over it, of course. When you fly over the ocean it looks all calm and sparkly, but it's very different down there at sea level!

BIG VOYAGES IN LITTLE SHIPS

You don't need a big ship to cross a big ocean. Small yachts may take longer, but if they're well equipped and can store enough supplies for an ocean crossing, why hurry?

Can't afford your own boat? No problem — hitch a ride on a boat needing crew. If you're good, you can make a career of it.

Sailing an ocean in small boats has never been safer — but you can never take the sea for granted. Even in warm tropical waters there are still storms and big waves occasionally. If you're really unlucky, you might even bump into a sleeping whale...

HAVING A WHALE OF A TIME

In 1973 the Robertson family were sailing across the Pacific Ocean in their schooner Lucette. They didn't see the whale just below the surface until it flicked its tail and sank their boat.

The family survived in a liferaft for nearly six weeks until they were rescued by a passing ship. Their supplies ran out after a few days but they managed to catch enough turtles and fish to keep themselves alive — just!

Oops, sorry!

AROUND THE WORLD — THE HARD WAY

If you want to sail round the world as fast as possible non stop, the shortest route is around the bottom of the world, through the wild and windy Southern Ocean. This is only a good idea if you love being cold, wet, shaken around in giant waves and doing without sleep, showers or decent food for weeks on end.

Surprisingly, not many people have experienced the wildest parts of the ocean this close up! On the next page we'll stow away on board with someone who has...

Mike Golding OBE, one of the world's top offshore sailors, has completed five round the world races so far, three of them solo. He is one of only a handful of people in the world to have experienced the wildest parts of the earth's oceans, so let's stow away on board Mike's Open 60 Ecover and find out what the Southern Ocean is really like ...

In the Atlantic there's plenty of wildlife around the boat — birds, dolphins and whales — but they get harder to spot the further south I go. The Southern Ocean is actually very rich in wildlife, but sightings are rare because there's so much space out there!

When the first wandering albatross appears, gliding above the swell with its four metre wingspan, I know that I'm reaching the real Southern Ocean.

The water of the Southern Ocean is cold and clear, reflecting the colours of the sky. On a stormy day the sea is grey and foreboding, but on sunny days the clear water sparkles.

It's an amazing place, wild and beautiful. You don't need to go there to appreciate how important it is to protect the oceans from harm. We need to understand how to change our behaviour on-shore, thousands of miles away, to keep the oceans safe and clean up the planet.

SAILING ALONE

For day after day, week after week, my whole world lies within the yacht's cabin and the unchanging horizon. Thanks to satellite phones and broadband I can keep in touch with family and friends and send them video images from the boat. But when I'm sailing fast through a freezing cold black stormy night, with only radar to help me avoid the unseen icebergs, it can be the loneliest place on earth.

Yes, dear, of course I'm remembering to wear my thermal vest...

GOING UP!

Climbing the mast at sea is something every single-handed sailor dreads, as the motion is much more extreme up there. Once I was repairing some damage 30 metres up when the weather turned nasty. I was thrown against the mast several times, once so hard it nearly knocked me out. I was shaking with fright and had a big gash in my head by the time I got safely down on deck!

Don't look down!

SHIP AHOY!

Occasionally I see other ships in the Southern Ocean, like warships on patrol, or survey ships on their way to the Antarctic. Even though we all have different reasons for being in such a lonely place, we always call up on the radio for a friendly chat. I also come across large factory fishing ships who don't stop for a chat — sadly, some of these are being used to hunt whales and other endangered creatures, sometimes in the name of research.

A BIT ABOUT THE BOAT...

Ecover is an Open 60, an 18 metre racing yacht (55 feet). She's very fast and light, but strong enough to cope with wild weather and enormous waves. Well, strong enough to cope with most things — Mike has been in such extreme weather that he's been dismasted twice!

Fish are good to eat; very nourishing and great with chips. The seas are full of them, almost the only creatures we still hunt in the wild for food. What could be more natural? But hang on — there are a few problems with the way we catch them...

NOT ENOUGH FISH IN THE SEA...

Fishing boats have become so much bigger and more efficient over the years that in some places they catch too many fish, leaving none to breed and replace stocks.

This is a problem for the oceans, as wiping out one kind of fish affects everything else in the ecosystem. It's also a problem for humans...

The Grand Banks off Newfoundland have been famous for cod fishing for centuries, but in 1992 it came to a stop — there were no more cod left. Thousands of fishermen were suddenly out of a job — and they're still waiting for the cod to come back.

NET PROFITS

Fishing nets used to have a wide mesh so that only the big tasty ones got caught and the baby ones swam safely through the holes so they could grow up and breed before being caught.

But as big fish get harder to find, the mesh on fishing nets has been getting smaller and smaller. Nothing escapes these fine mesh nets, and everything that isn't needed is thrown back dead. Fish that are too small to eat are turned into animal food or fertiliser.

Fish can't swim backwards very easily! Once they're in the net, they're stuck.

BYE-BYE CATCH...
Everything accidentally caught in these massive modern nets is called by-catch, and it's not just the small stuff that suffers. Thousands of sea mammals like dolphins, porpoises and even albatross die every year when caught in nets.

Is that the 'internet' they're all talking about?

What do you call a fish with no eyes?

A FSH!

WHAT'S THE ANSWER?
Governments are getting stricter about imposing limits on how much fish are allowed to be caught, and areas that have run out have to be allowed to recover. With careful management and attention to correct mesh sizes, fishing stocks can be managed so that they are a constant source of food for both humans and animals forever...

What can you do to help? You don't have to give up eating fish. The Good Fish Guide tells you which fish are sustainably caught, turn to page 95 for details.

FAIRY COD-MOTHER

THE AMAZING ALBATROSS

The wandering albatross, with a wingspan of up to four metres, is the largest and most impressive seabird of all. The albatross spends most of its life on the ocean and can even sleep on the surface of the water.

Because they travel so far in search of food, a mother albatross will swallow the food she finds for her chick and then sick it up again when she gets back to her nest.

Yummy... Lunch!

There is a superstition that the albatross is the soul of a dead sailor and it used to be considered bad luck to kill one. Unfortunately, the superstition seems to have died out, which the albatross is also in danger of doing...

THE REAL ALBERT ROSS

Unless you sail the wildest parts of the ocean, your chances of seeing an albatross are small, especially as most of them live in the Southern Hemisphere.

Think I should have turned right at the Falklands...

But for 20 years, a lone black-browed albatross lived for part of each year on his own ledge amongst a gannet colony on the Shetlands. Locals and birdwatchers called him Albert Ross and were sad when he finally disappeared in 1996.

The Good Fish Guide will tell you which tinned fish like tuna are caught by non-harmful methods.

So spread the word!

THE PROBLEM...

A popular fishing technique is called long-lining, which, as you'd guess, involves a boat trailing miles and miles of fishing line with lots of hooks on it. The problem is that albatross and other seabirds dive on the hooked fish, get stuck on the hooks and drown. Over 100,000 birds a year die in this way.

Yummy... lunch!

... THE SOLUTION

The RSPB has joined forces with bird protection groups from around the world to take action before it's too late. They have set up the Albatross Task Force, teams of people who go direct to the fishermen and teach them ways of fishing that don't harm seabirds. It can be as simple as trailing a line of colourful streamers to frighten the birds away, or making sure the fishing line sinks lower into the water.

What can you do to help? For a few pounds you can buy a long-lining kit or bird identification kit from the RSPB. Don't worry, the kits don't come to your house, they go straight to where they're needed!

THANK YOU

When plastic was first invented early in the 20th century, everybody thought it was a brilliant idea. By the last few decades of the century, it had taken over almost every aspect of life. What useful stuff, how clever...

... OR PERHAPS NOT SO CLEVER

The problem with plastic is that it lasts. It lasts forever — well, thousands of years at least. There's no way to get rid of it. Burning it emits toxic gas, so that's not a sensible option.

This means that almost every piece of plastic ever made is still with us. Look around you — how many plastic things can you see? We're so used to it, we don't notice it any more.

GUESS WHERE IT ENDS UP?

Most goes to landfill, some gets recycled. But the rest ends up in the water or dropped in the street, where it gets blown by the wind, carried down rivers and into the sea.

Yummy... lunch!

Bodies of dead seabirds are found full of plastic; baby birds are fed pieces of plastic by their parents and then die of starvation. How are they to know that something floating in the sea is not good to eat? Animals and fish get tangled up in rubbish and die. Turtles eat floating plastic thinking it's a tasty snack. Over a million birds and animals die each year through eating or getting tangled up in rubbish. It's a big problem.

HOW BIG??

Remember those ocean gyres — the big circulating currents of water? They scoop up all the floating junk that finds its way into the sea and collect it together in the middle — and there it stays. The biggest is in the north Pacific, which in 2010 was thought to be almost as big as western Europe, and still growing fast.

Scientists are keeping an eye on rubbish patches in other oceans — the north Atlantic now has its own, and there are others. Time for action!

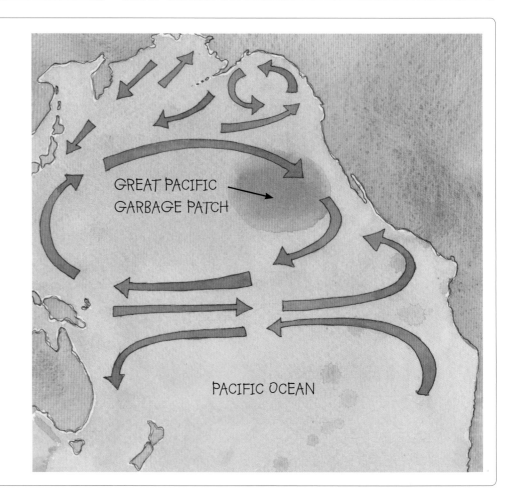

GREAT PACIFIC GARBAGE PATCH

PACIFIC OCEAN

OUT OF SIGHT, OUT OF MIND?

You can't solve a problem until people know it exists. The Plastiki is a catamaran made entirely from recycled plastic — the hulls are made from 12,000 plastic bottles and the sails are recycled PET plastic. The boat set sail from San Francisco in spring 2010 to raise environmental awareness of the problem of plastic waste.

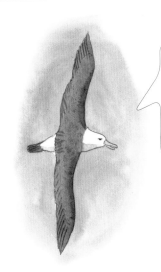

DON'T THROW IT AWAY!
There is no more 'Away'... Later in the book there is plenty of advice on what you can do to help stop waste.

PLASTIC PLANKTON

Plastic rubbish breaks down into smaller and smaller pieces until it becomes tiny particles suspended in the water — a kind of plastic chemical soup. It's now possible that there is more plastic in the sea than plankton!

Some of that chemical soup ends up inside fish, of course, and gets into the food chain.

And guess who eats some of that fish? That's right — you and me...

Eat up your fish — it's good for you!

Nobody knows for sure how many plastic chemicals are getting into your fish and chips, but it's food for thought — and it's not the fish's fault!

WE WERE CLEVER ENOUGH TO GET INTO A MESS... LET'S BE CLEVER ENOUGH TO GET OUT OF IT!

Plastic is made from oil, which is gradually becoming more expensive. Big companies are already using science to find new ways of making plastic out of other things — plastics which are fully biodegradable and won't mess up the planet.

And here's a clever idea — how about turning plastic back into oil and using it for energy? This research is in its early stages, but perhaps the next generation of scientists (that's you!) will be the ones using plastic waste from the oceans to heat your homes.

Oil and gas took millions of years to form, compressed in layers of rock, but we've used most of it up within a century. Oil companies are going further out to sea and digging deeper to find it, but this brings its own problems and the oil won't last forever.

But the constantly moving oceans hold the promise of plenty of sustainable energy... all we need is the technology to capture it.

THE WIND IS FREE

Clusters of giant wind turbines are being sited out to sea, where the wind blows uninterrupted by hills or buildings, and out of sight of land. Their size and bright yellow colour should ensure that ships don't bump into them!

TIDAL ENERGY

Tidal energy projects usually need to be close to the coast where tides are strongest. Even slow moving currents can generate useful amounts of power — and unlike the wind, the tide can be relied upon!

'WAVE' GOODBYE TO OIL AND GAS...

Wave energy has great potential as a source of power. Several weird and wonderful inventions are being developed to harness the movement of the ocean's swell and turn it into electricity... inventions like these:

WAVE SNAKES are designed to convert the motion of the waves into power through the movement of hinged joints on connected cylinders.

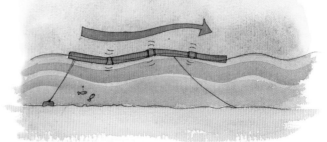

The wave snake is moored to the seabed so that it will always lie head on to the waves. Each section is about the size of a railway carriage.

WAVE CATCHERS funnel the waves so that the water pours into a reservoir which is at a higher level to the sea. The trapped water has to go past turbines to get back to the sea, and the turbines generate electricity.

Every wave flops more water into the wave catcher's reservoir.

ALL AT SEA

You don't have to sail far out into the open ocean to get a feel for the sea and everything that lives in it. Even close to shore, life at sea is as different as it can possibly be from life on land. You can come and enjoy it, but never ever forget you are just visitors to our world!

Every sailor knows about tides, but do you know what causes them? The sun and the moon between them have enough gravity to pull all the water in the oceans into a *bulge* twice a day. The moon may be small compared to the sun, but because it's so close to us its pull is strong.

As the moon travels round the planet it pulls the water into a bulge twice every 24 hours. About twice a month the sun and moon are in a line, so the pull is even stronger, which makes the tides more extreme — spring tides. When the moon and sun are no longer lined up, the pull is weaker — neap tides. This is how it works:

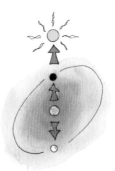 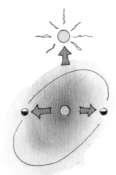

SPRING TIDES happen at a new and full moon when the sun and moon are pulling in the same direction.

NEAP TIDES happen at a half moon and are not as strong as spring tides.

The difference between high and low water is called the TIDAL RANGE. Spring tides go higher and lower than neap tides, so the tidal range is greater.

The movement of water up and down the coast is called the TIDAL STREAM. If you're sailing, you'll wait for a free ride on a strong tide rather than try to sail against it.

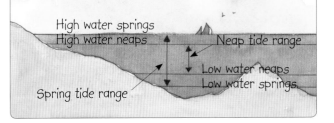

High water springs
High water neaps
Neap tide range
Low water neaps
Low water springs
Spring tide range

IN A WHIRL...

In some places, strong tides squeezed around headlands or islands can cause a whirlpool or maelstrom. Off the west coast of Scotland, the Corryvreckan is the third largest whirlpool in the world, with waves up to 9m high. The roar of the water can be heard up to ten miles away.

HIGH AND DRY

Out in deep water the movement of tides is too small to notice, but when land gets in the way, it's a different story. The shape of the land and rise in the sea floor force the water to move further and faster to get round it.

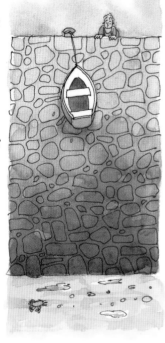

The biggest tidal range in the world is found in the Bay of Fundy in Newfoundland, where the difference between high and low water can be up to 17 metres.

In Europe, the prize for the biggest tides goes to the Bristol Channel on the west coast of the UK which get up to 15 metres.

Find out more about how tides affect the coast in Chapter Four

Everyone is familiar with the litter-loving herring gull, but there are many different types of amazing sea birds to look out for around north European and UK waters. If you're out on the water or on the coast, see how many you can recognise...

BLACK-BACKED GULL

One of the largest gulls, easy to spot in winter when large numbers are found on rocky coasts and islands.

GANNET

Large graceful birds found close to rocky cliffs. Look out for flocks of gannets diving for fish — they fold their wings back and drop like a rocket from a great height. Impressive!

PUFFIN

A small bird but easy to recognise with its colourful beak and short stubby wings. Visits rocky shores in the summer to build a nest in burrows, but spends winters far out to sea.

FULMAR

Related to albatrosses, fulmars are part of a family called tubenoses because of the tube shaped nostril on top of the beak which helps get rid of excess salt. Spends most of its life at sea, but comes ashore to breed on high cliffs.

TERN

Small birds sometimes called the swallows of the sea because of their long tail feathers. The Arctic tern covers an impressive distance every year as it spends summer in northern Europe but winters in Antarctica!

CORMORANT

A large bird found on rocky coasts. It floats very low in the water, so that you often only see the neck sticking out above the waves. Cormorants' wings are not waterproof like other birds, so they often sit on a rock with their wings spread out to dry.

RAZORBILL

Razorbills and guillemots look quite similar from a distance, but the razorbill is a bit smaller and has a distinctive blunt bill with a white band.

GUILLEMOT

Flocks of guillemot bob up and down on the sea like corks, occasionally diving for fish. You can tell them apart from Razorbills, because when they fly, their feet stick out beyond their tails.

MANX SHEARWATER

Lives well out to sea, only coming ashore to breed. You'll see it flying low over the water, or gliding in high winds, flashing black and white in turn as it shows the tops and then the bottoms of its wings.

KITTIWAKE

A small, pretty gull which gets its name from its call which sounds like 'Kitt-ee-wake'. It spends all of its life at sea, only coming ashore to breed.

LESSER-SPOTTED WILDLIFE WATCHER

Keep a good bird book handy so you can find out which bird is which. Keep a scrapbook with photos, notes and sketches of everything you see.

Practise using binoculars to get a close up view of sea life.

Remember always to put the strap around your neck.

Well I can't see it anywhere!

Don't just use your eyes — use your ears to listen to and learn to recognise different bird calls.

BLACK-HEADED GULL

A small and pretty gull, often found squabbling over scraps around the harbour. In winter, the black colour on the head changes to white with a black smudge behind the eye.

Think that throwing rubbish into the water doesn't really matter? Think again! Human carelessness causes big problems for sea life and over a million birds die every year from getting tangled in rubbish or eating it. It all needs taking back to shore. Yes, that's right — all of it!

Important message from Tina Tern...

You don't have to sail far to spot sea mammals, especially dolphins and porpoises. They like playing in a boat's bow wave and it's always exciting when they do. Whales, dolphins and porpoises are all called cetaceans — can you tell them apart?

DOLPHINS

There are more than 20 different types of dolphin, but these two are the ones you're most likely to spot in coastal waters. They grow up to 3 metres and swim in pods of up to 25. They are highly intelligent, acrobatic and playful creatures, leaping high out of the water just for fun, and riding on your boat's bow wave if you're lucky. Like whales, they have a blowhole to breathe air, which closes when they dive underwater.

When asleep, only half the dolphin's brain sleeps at a time, so one half is always awake enough for the dolphin to rise up to the surface to breathe!

BOTTLENOSE DOLPHIN

Blowhole

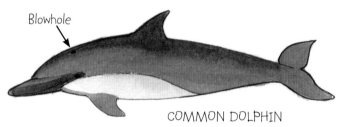

COMMON DOLPHIN

PILOT WHALE

Is really a type of dolphin, but grows up to 8 metres long so it is quite impressive. Like other dolphins, pilot whales have strong family bonds and travel in large pods.

HARBOUR PORPOISE

Smaller than dolphins, with a blunt nose and smaller dorsal fin. Porpoises are less likely than dolphins to leap out of the water, so you'll probably see just the back and fin.

Having a whale of a time?

SEALS

Grey seals are the easiest to spot around UK waters. At up to 3 metres (9 feet) long, they're larger than common seals, which actually aren't that common! So how can you tell them apart? The common seal has a mottled grey or brown coat and a blunt face. The grey seal is a more even dark grey colour and has a longer face. When you see a grey seal in the water, it's easy to mistake it for a dog!

COMMON SEAL

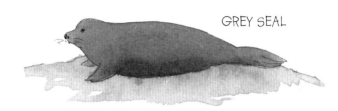

GREY SEAL

BASKING SHARK

This is a fish not a mammal, but it's so big — up to 12 metres (40 feet) long — that you might well see it when you're on the lookout for dolphins or whales. It's the second largest fish in the world, and can be seen around UK coasts in the summer, when it likes to rest near the surface of the water on hot sunny days. It has an enormous mouth which looks very scary but in fact these gentle giants eat only plankton.

MINKE WHALE

Up to 9 metres (27 feet) long, here's another whale you might be lucky enough to see in north European waters.

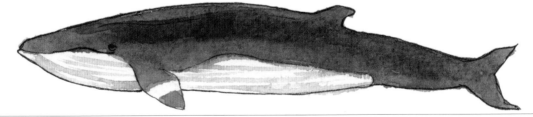

LEATHERBACK TURTLE

Here's something special — up to 3 metres (9 feet) long, the turtle is a summer visitor to UK waters, but sadly now very rare. There are so few left that the turtle is considered critically endangered.

Find out on the next page how to get close to marine animals without scaring us off...

Marine mammals and basking sharks are protected in UK waters, which means that if you intentionally cause them stress or damage, you're breaking the law... but who would want to do that? Seeing these creatures close up is a fantastic experience, and here's what to do to make the most of it.

WILDLIFE RULES!

 If you keep a constant speed and direction, dolphins are more likely to approach and play on your bow wave. Five knots or less is ideal.

 Never, ever chase them.

 Avoid coming between a mother and her young, or steering through the middle of a group.

 Avoid erratic behaviour, noise and sudden changes of speed or you'll frighten them away.

 Resist the temptation to call up other boats to have a look as this will distress the animals and they'll disappear.

 Don't try to swim with, touch, or feed the animals.

 Basking sharks and whales are particularly vulnerable to damage from boats' propellers. If they swim close to your boat put the engine into neutral. Remember that they travel in groups, so there will be more below the surface that you can't see.

 Don't forget to take photographs! (but avoid using the flash).

Sightings of basking sharks and turtles should be reported to the Marine Conservation Society (www.mcs.org).

Funny, it's almost as if they can talk to each other!

Dolphins use echolocation to see with sound. They make a series of clicking sounds at different frequencies which bounce off objects that are out of sight. The returning echo from their clicks tells them what's ahead of them and where shoals of fish are.

It is also possible that the dolphins use these clicks and squeaks to communicate with each other.

Some parts of the sea and coast are so special that they are protected by law to keep them that way. These places are generally called Marine Protected Areas. In the UK they also have names like Special Area of Conservation (SAC), Site of Special Scientific Interest (SSSI), or Marine Conservation Zone (MCZ), but the theme of them all is care and respect.

Marine reserves and other protected areas are great to visit. Whether you're in your own boat or a passenger on a tour boat, they all have rules for visitors to follow. This is not to stop you having fun but to make sure that human visitors don't spoil what makes these places special..

Yes, they migrate here in large numbers at this time of year.

Find out as much as you can *before* you visit. Some areas are particularly sensitive at certain times of the year, for example when young animals are being born.

Unlike inland birds, seabirds don't have trees to make their nests in! So they have to use rocky ledges, grassy cliff tops or amongst the reeds in marshes.

MOORING MANNERS

The sea bed beneath your keel is just as protected as the land above. Make sure that you don't anchor in a place where anchoring is forbidden. If it is, it's for a good reason — delicate reefs or rare types of grass on the sea bed will be damaged when your great big lump of metal lands on them!

Most places will have visitors' moorings available so you don't have to anchor, but if necessary go and anchor somewhere else and explore by dinghy.

LANDING MANNERS

If you go ashore on a marine reserve, check before you head off for the nearest beach as there may be restrictions on where you can land. Most marine reserves will have a special landing place where you can safely go ashore. Don't forget the binoculars.

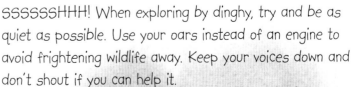

SSSSSSHHH! When exploring by dinghy, try and be as quiet as possible. Use your oars instead of an engine to avoid frightening wildlife away. Keep your voices down and don't shout if you can help it.

It's not just marine mammals who need respect — there's a whole world below the surface that should be treated with care. Just because you can't see what's down there doesn't mean you can mess it up!

TOILET TROUBLES

When using the toilet at anchor, use the boat's holding tank if there is one. Only empty tanks at pump-out facilities or far offshore where waste is quickly dispersed. Flushing out close to shore or in sheltered bays contaminates the sea and depletes oxygen levels that sea life depends on — and going for a swim in poo is not very nice for humans either!

Um... those funny brown fish you told me about...

CHEMICAL SOUP

Most detergents and cleaning products contain chemicals, so it's a good idea to use environmentally friendly products wherever you can.

A LOAD OF RUBBISH!

Don't throw anything into the water, not even if it's biodegradable. Sometimes the wind can blow plastic bags and wrappers overboard, so it's a good idea to unwrap your lunch below deck. The plastic rings that link drinks cans together are particularly nasty for birds who get horribly tangled up in them.

OIL AND WATER DON'T MIX!

Don't let any drops of fuel or oil spill into the sea when refuelling the outboard. You may think a few drops don't matter, but collectively they add up to a big problem. More about this in the next chapter...

SOMETHING FISHY GOING ON?

If you like fish for your supper, there's nothing better than catching it yourself. But before you throw your line over the side, make sure you're not in a NO TAKE ZONE.

No Take Zones were set up in a few places to ban fishing completely and prevent fish stocks becoming dangerously low. This may sound like bad news for fishermen, but at Lundy Island in the Bristol Channel the lobster population has increased so much within the No Take Zone that they're spilling over into places where they can be caught. Good news for both lobsters and fishermen.

When you do catch fish, take only what you need to eat and always throw the little ones back so they can grow big and be caught another day.

It's not just what you do on your boat that affects the seas — at the end of the book you'll find out how your actions at home make a difference too.

THANK YOU

What lives below the surface of the sea apart from fish? Well there are thousands of different species, some of them so weird you can't tell if they're plants or animals. If you get the chance to go snorkelling or swimming, here are a few of the things you may see. Believe it or not, these are all animals!

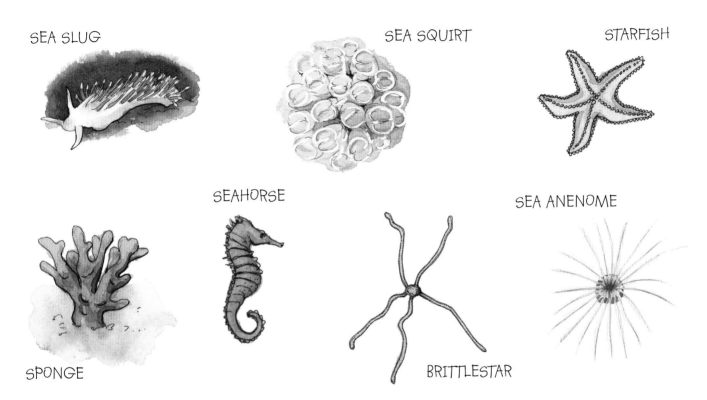

SEA SLUG

SEA SQUIRT

STARFISH

SEAHORSE

SEA ANENOME

SPONGE

BRITTLESTAR

DOWN ON THE SEA BED...

There are forests, grassy plains, deserts and mountains on the sea bed just like there are on land.

KELP, the biggest type of seaweed and it is the forest of the sea bed, its thick trunks and dense fronds are a home and hiding place for hundreds of tiny creatures.

EEL GRASS, is a very special plant, providing meadows for seahorses and a nursery for baby fish who hide amongst the grass where big hungry fish can't see them.

Come on out, I know you're in there!

DIVE IN!

Snorkelling or diving in clear water is like visiting a whole new world. Remember that it belongs to the creatures that live there — you are just a visitor. Try not to touch anything if you can help it, not just because some plants and animals like sea urchins may sting you, but because corals in particular are very delicate and will die if touched.

Don't try and collect any souvenirs — unless you stumble across shipwrecked treasure of course!

There are lots of do's and don'ts in this chapter, but now you know why they're so important, it's a good idea to put them all onto one list. Make your own Marine Code of Conduct for your boat and the area you sail in — something like this...

One good tern deserves another!

Marine code for "(boat name)" and her crew:

We do not throw anything overboard, but take all our rubbish back to shore and dispose of it properly.

We only use cleaning products which are natural and biodegradable.

We use our boat's holding tanks when close to shore and in sheltered waters, and only empty them when well offshore or at proper pump-out facilities ashore.

Before anchoring, we make sure we're not in a no anchoring zone.

We only fill our fuel tanks on board or in the dinghy using gear designed to avoid any spills.

We keep to a slow speed close to shore and close to wildlife.

We don't take any more fish than we need, and put back all smaller ones.

We check for seasonal restrictions in sensitive areas to avoid disturbing young birds or seals.

Signed: . . . . (Skipper) . . . . (Crew)

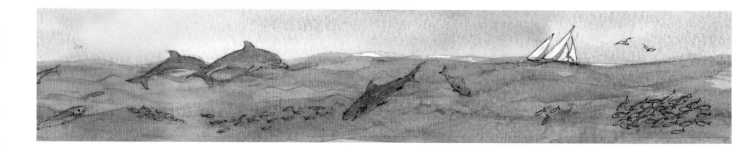

ON THE EDGE

The place where land and sea meet is special, both for animals and humans.

There are all sorts of coastlines, from wild and rocky to soft and soggy, but they all need looking after.

CHLOE CRAB

Coastlines come in all shapes and size, and like everything else on the planet, they're always changing. Crumbly, low lying coastlines change faster than hard rocky ones — and it's not always the sea that wins!

COASTLINE CRUMBLE

Crumbly coastlines can get nibbled away by the sea amazingly quickly. On the east coast of England there are places where the coast is disappearing at the rate of two metres a year. During a storm in 1967 six metres of coast was washed away from Holderness in Yorkshire!

FOR SALE... Sea views, four bedrooms — oops, I mean two bedrooms...

GOING DOWN!

If the sea level changes, so does the landscape. At the end of the last ice age when melting ice made sea levels rise, river estuaries became flooded and are now called RIAS.

In a very mountainous area like Norway, these flooded estuaries became fabulous fjords, but you can also find them in the UK on a smaller scale, like Salcombe or the deep water harbour of Milford Haven in Wales.

LAND FIGHTS BACK

But the sea doesn't have it all its own way. Some coastlines are growing, especially if the wave action is quiet enough for the sea to dump its sand and silt rather than bash out more. River estuaries also bring silt and mud down from inland to add to the process.

The town of Sandwich in Kent used to be an important port, but now it's two miles inland — and it's not the town that's moved! A big storm in the 13th century deposited lots of sand across the entrance to the river, which was added to over the following centuries.

The sea? It's moved, mate — about 2 miles that way...

GOING UP!

It's not just the sea level that rises — the land does it too sometimes. In some places the land was so relieved that the weight of all that ice had gone that it rose up, giving raised beaches.

OLD BEACH

NEW BEACH

Where does the coastline end and the sea begin? The line on an Ordnance Survey map shows the edge of the land at high tide, but the space between high and low water is sometimes land and sometimes sea. This is called the inter-tidal zone, and there are some very strange and very clever creatures living there.

THE INTER-TIDAL ZONE

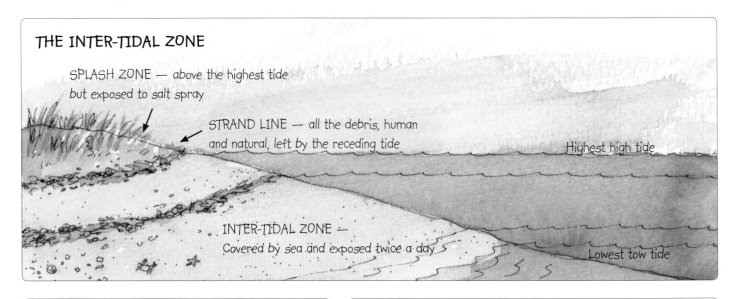

SPLASH ZONE — above the highest tide but exposed to salt spray

STRAND LINE — all the debris, human and natural, left by the receding tide

INTER-TIDAL ZONE — Covered by sea and exposed twice a day

Highest high tide

Lowest tow tide

DON'T GET TIDE UP!

If you don't have wings, don't get caught by the tide. If you're going to the beach check the times of high and low water, especially in rocky coves that can get cut off by the tide.

SURF'S NOT UP...

Some coastlines have a much higher tidal range than others. On a gently shelving beach the tide will also appear to come in really quickly — so don't get caught out just because the sea looks a long way away.

Do you know how to read a tide table? It will help you make the most of your visit to the beach.

There are usually two high tides and two low tides each day.

Check the height column to find out which are the highs and which are the lows.

LOW WATER
HIGH WATER
LOW WATER
HIGH WATER

Date	Time h.m.	Height m	ft	Range m	ft
1	0242	1·5	4·8	4·9	16·3
Tu	0845	6·0	19·8	4·5	15·0
	1455	1·7	5·5	4·3	14·3
	2104	6·2	20·3	4·5	14·8

The tidal RANGE shows you the difference between high and low tide. So a spring tide has a big range which means the tide will come in higher and go out further than a neap tide.

'WATCH' OUT! Some tide tables are all based on GMT, but there will be a note at the bottom of the page to tell you if you need to add an hour for British Summer Time.

Coastlines are shaped by waves; big and powerful or soft and gentle. Before rushing into the water with your surfboard, let's have a look at where waves come from and what happens when they bump into the land...

HOW WAVES WORK

Waves are driven by the wind, but what moves forward is not water, but energy. Each drop of water swirls in a circle as the wave passes through it. The distance a wave has travelled across an ocean is called the fetch.

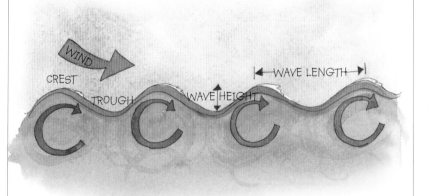

Things change when a lump of land gets in the way. As the bottom of the wave bumps into the land, the wave trips over itself and falls flat on its face — giving surfers a good time along the way if it's a nice big one!

Friction slows down the bottom of the wave

As the wave breaks the water is carried up the beach — this is called the SWASH. The water running back into the sea again is called the BACKWASH. If you stand at the edge of the waves you can feel the force of water and sand running backwards around your feet.

If the land shelves gently, the wave energy will be scattered well away from the shore. If the water is deep close to the shore, waves come all the way in before they break. Steep shores plus a long fetch can bring some really big waves!

THE WORLD'S BIGGEST WAVES

If you want to find big waves you need a coastline facing an ocean, with onshore winds and a shelving beach.

The coasts of the Pacific Ocean have the longest fetch and the biggest waves. The highest ever recorded was 34 metres (110 feet) high!

When the seabed is shallower at one end of the beach than the other, the wave breaks over the shallow part first, causing a huge gradually breaking 'barrel' — the ultimate surfing ride.

What did one ocean say to the other?

Nothing, it just gave a little wave!

From *big* ports to little harbours, seaside towns and cities are *busy* places. Wherever there's human activity, there's waste and rubbish, so we need to take extra care to make sure our impact is as low as possible.

Most harbours and marinas have recycling centres and special disposal bins for toxic waste.

Use the shoreside toilets or holding tanks when in harbour.

Is your bottom mucky? (the *boat's*, not yours...). If you're scrubbing and painting your boat, see if the marina has a closed loop system which stops poisonous antifouling paint being washed into the water. Dispose of all rags and brushes carefully.

Some antifoul paints are less damaging to the environment than others — help your skipper to choose one that's not going to give sea life a tummy ache!

Only about 5% of oil pollution comes from big disasters like a tanker on the rocks. The rest is all down to lots of people not being careful enough when handling fuels and oil on board boats. When refuelling a small boat or outboard, use a big enough funnel, don't over-fill, mop up spills, and get rid of old engine oil carefully.

Going fishing? Make sure your lines and nets don't get left behind or dropped into the sea — they cause a lot of damage to wildlife.

Whether you're visiting a harbour by land or by sea, dispose of your litter carefully and don't be careless with your ice cream wrappers.

Ice cream? Yummy!

Don't feed the seagulls — human food and rubbish isn't good for them!

Harbours and jetties are great for crabbing — but have you ever thought about it from the crabs' point of view?

If crabs could have their say, their advice to crabbers might go something like this...

CHLOE CRAB'S GUIDE TO HAPPY CRABBING

 Never use a barbed crabbing line. If you buy one with a sharp hook on it, please cut it off. Then either tie the bait onto the string, or put it in one of those small net bags that washing tabs come in (having rinsed it first to get all the soap out).

 Bacon pieces make good bait, or any small scraps of meat.

 Handle us carefully — how would you like it if someone pulled your legs or arms off? Use a net to transfer us to your bucket of water.

 Put plenty of sea water in the bucket and don't leave us exposed to the hot sun for too long. Keep refreshing the water in the bucket so we don't run out of oxygen.

 Put us carefully back into the water when you've finished.

 Take care when crabbing from a pontoon or pier as boats may need to come alongside.

 Wear a lifejacket when crabbing near deep water.

 Never ever leave your crabbing line behind or throw it in the water. Always take it home with you, even if it's tangled up and a bit smelly.

CRABBY FACTS

- A crab's teeth are in its stomach.
- Crabs breathe underwater using gills, but they can survive for long periods out of the water as long as they stay cool and their gills don't dry out.
- The world's biggest crab? The Japanese spider crab grows up to four metres across!
- When a crab grows out of its shell, it breaks it open and then hides to stay safe while a new one forms.

THANKS!

Whether you're into surfing, swimming, paddling, kayaking, building sandcastles or just lazing around, you can't beat a nice sandy beach. But there's more to a beach than a pile of sand, and beaches with rocky bits are well worth looking into...

THE WONDERFUL WORLD OF ROCKPOOLS

Take a close look at pools and the rocks in the inter-tidal zone. There are creatures living there so weird that if they weren't so small you'd think they'd landed from another planet.

Think about their world. How would you cope being sloshed by cold waves one minute and boiled by the sun the next? Half the time you're under water, half the time you're high and dry. Here are just a few of the amazing creatures who can survive this type of environment...

SEA ANENOME

Animals that look a bit like flowers, you'll find anemones in rockpools. They cling tightly to rocks so they can't get off to chase food. They use their long tentacles to sting and paralyse any small creatures that drift past. When they're not underwater, they draw their tentacles in and look like a red blob waiting for the tide to come in.

HERMIT CRAB

These crabs have no hard shell of their own, so to avoid getting eaten they move into another creature's empty shell. You'll find them at the bottom of rockpools with just their claws sticking out.

SHRIMP

Shrimps are very common in rockpools, but they're small and almost see-through, so very hard to spot. Sometimes you'll see their shadow darting around on the bottom of the rockpool before you see the shrimp itself.

SEA SPIDER

Quite hard to spot, sea spiders can be found amongst seaweed and hiding under rocks.

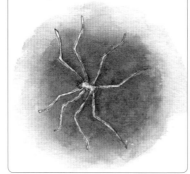

BREADCRUMB SPONGE

You'll find this in rockpools and attached to rocks, but if you squeeze it, it smells of rotting seaweed. Yeuk!

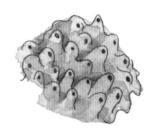

CLEVER DIGGERS

Creatures living in the sand take a dive downwards when the tide goes out, so you probably won't spot them. But if you know what to look for you can *see* the trails they leave behind...

LUGWORM

It's easy to spot the swirly cast left by the lugworm, who eats the sand as it tunnels down and leaves this heap of sand behind. Look for the little hollow in the sand close to the cast, as that tells you where the worm's head is.

SAND MASON

If you see small sandy tubes with branched tops sticking out of the sand, these are made by sand mason worms who burrow vertically into the sand. The worms have fine tentacles which stick out of the top of the tube to catch their food.

CLEVER CLINGERS

Creatures that don't move very much need to be able to cling on tight to their rock when the tide leaves them high and dry.

LIMPETS cling to rocks with very powerful suction. They move around at night to feed off algae, but always return to exactly the same place on their rock. They start life as boys but usually change into girls after a few years!

BARNACLES open up at the top when the tide comes in and catch plankton with their feathery feet. They keep their lids firmly shut when out of the water.

LIMPET

BARNACLE

BAKED BEANS AND POTATOES? These strange animals may sound tasty, but don't try to eat them!

The baked bean sea squirt gets its name because it really does look like a pile of baked beans, but don't try to eat it! Look for sea squirts under rocky ledges and other cool dark places.

The sea potato is covered with small spines that it uses to burrow under the sand. It's related to the starfish, and if you find a dried shell of a sea potato on the sand it will have a star shape on it.

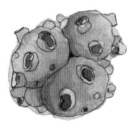

Seashore creatures are very easily damaged — even me! — so if you want to catch rockpool animals in your net, handle us very carefully. Put us back gently where you found us when it's time to go home.

Collecting treasures from the seashore is something most of us like to do. Shells, driftwood, feathers and other cast-offs can all be taken home with you — but remember to give everything a wash in freshwater to stop it getting smelly and do not take too many!

SHELLS are everyone's favourite, in all sorts of shapes and colours. Here are some of the most common...

OYSTER

LIMPET

PERIWINKLE

SPINY COCKLE

MUSSEL

TOWER SHELL

BANDED WEDGE SHELL

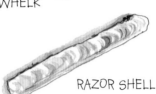
WHELK

RAZOR SHELL

IMPORTANT — only take shells that are no longer lived in! If there's still a creature living inside, put it back where you found it.

HANDS OFF!

OTHER SHORELINE TREASURES

Some are man-made, like bleached driftwood. Some are animal cast-offs like crab shells or feathers. Keep your eyes open for some unusual finds.

EMPTY CRAB CASE — the crab has outgrown it!

BIT OF ROPE — gets hairy!

MERMAID'S PURSE — an empty skate eggs case

Driftwood — both natural and man made, gets bleached and sculpted by the waves

NOT SO NICE...

Have you noticed how much plastic is lying around on the strand line? It's washed up by the sea, blown in by the wind, and dropped by careless people. If you live near the coast, join in a local beach clean, which is good fun as well as a great way to pay back the beach for all the fun it gives you.

Thanks!

Every year, in the third weekend of September, the Marine Conservation Society organises a Beachwatch Big Weekend all around the UK.

HOW TO BE BEACH SMART...

 Never leave litter, take it all home with you, every single bit. Leave only footprints behind you.

 If you have a barbecue or bonfire, use a disposable barbecue so you can take the remains home with you.

 Put everything back where you found it — if you turn rocks over to see what lives underneath, put them back again in the same position.

 Take care when handling rockpool creatures or crabs, as they are easily damaged.

 Don't trample through rockpools or throw stones into them — you wouldn't like it if someone threw rocks at your home!

 Don't take anything home that's alive. Collect shells — but not if they're still lived in.

 Always check tide times to make the most of your day on the beach. Rockpooling and exploring are best when the tide is going out. Swimming can be best when the tide is coming in over warm sand. Don't get cut off by the incoming tide.

 Join a local or national beach clean scheme to help keep your favourite beaches beautiful.

 If you find a stranded whale or dolphin on the beach, dead or alive, don't touch it, but contact the RSPCA as soon as possible.

 Avoid buying shells, starfish or other marine creatures from souvenir shops — they are likely to have been collected when alive.

Check local rules before taking your dog on the beach — and always clean up after it.

Well really... what does he think beaches are for?

In low lying areas where river estuaries drop plenty of mud and sediment into the sea, the landscape is less dramatic. Instead of waves crashing onto rocks, sea and land are so closely merged that it's hard to see where one ends and the other begins...

JUST A LOAD OF OLD MUD?

To human eyes, a low lying marshy coast is nowhere near as much fun as a sandy beach. But remember, the coast isn't there just for our benefit! Salt marshes give birds and animals a safe place to live and breed.

Marshland has an important job to do for humans too. They protect the land from erosion by forming a barrier that can absorb the sea, and the plants growing in the salt marsh stop the mud from being washed away.

EXPLORING BY LAND

If you go for a walk on low lying coasts, take care! Mud can be very soft and deep, and people do get stuck sometimes. If you get stuck and then the tide comes in, you're in big trouble...

Next time... no more short cuts!

Remember to check your tide tables!

EXPLORING BY BOAT

If visiting tidal creeks by small boat, plan your trip around the tides. In many creeks and tidal backwaters, the tide goes out a lot quicker than it comes in!

Keep your speed low to avoid damaging the banks with your wash, or churning up the sediment underwater. Engine noise can stress birds and animals, especially if they are looking after their babies, so if you make a noise you'll see nothing.

If you need to use an engine, have a look at electric ones which are almost silent — perfect for quiet waters. Better still, if the creeks are too narrow to sail, get the oars out or use a canoe.

No, you get out and push!

TEE HEE

Salt marshes may look like a lot of boggy mud to you, but they're full of life, with plenty of sheltered water for young fish to grow. Birds think saltings are brilliant places to live — plenty of space to raise a family and lots of free restaurants close by. What could be better? So put on your wellies, take the binoculars and let's take a look...

TURNSTONE

Look out for these small birds on rocky shores as well as muddy ones, as they like to pick small insects and crustaceans from rocks.

OYSTER-CATCHER

A distinctive black and white bird with orange/red beak and a short piercing call. Oyster-catchers live on mussels and cockles, prising the shells open with their strong beak.

CURLEW

A large bird living on wetlands and estuaries, the curlew has a loud and distinctive call. It has a long curved beak to dig into the mud at low tide and find worms, shrimps and other small creatures to eat.

SANDERLING

Look for these small winter visitors running busily about at the water's edge, chasing waves and looking in the mud or sand for small creatures to eat.

LITTLE EGRET

Flocks of these small white herons can be seen in estuaries, hunting for fish. These elegant birds used to be very rare, but they are now found in quite large numbers.

It's easy to see when a sandy beach with clear water is polluted, but muddy waters have a problem — they look mucky even when the mud is clean and healthy! Don't chuck your rubbish in the mud — it causes damage, even when you can't see it!

More than half the world's population lives by the sea — it's our favourite place to work and play. We've always needed to find ways to hold the sea back and stop it eating away at the land, but with sea levels gradually rising we need to get even smarter about how we protect our coastlines.

One: HARD DEFENCES

Hard defences like concrete breakwaters are designed to keep the sea back by giving the waves a wall of concrete or rocks to break against.

Hee hee hee, you can't splash me!

There are many different types. If you want some new words to impress your family, try **gabion** (piles of rocks held in place with metal cages) and **riprap** (layers of rocks with the heaviest boulders on top).

Verdict: This method works — but it has a few drawbacks. It's expensive, doesn't last forever, and we can't concrete the entire coastline!

Two: THE KING CANUTE METHOD

The story goes that in the tenth century King Canute set his throne on the sea shore and commanded the tide not to come any closer and wet his feet. You can guess what happened next.

Verdict: Hmmm, not such a good idea after all.

Three: SOFT DEFENCES

Beach nourishment: This means bringing lorry loads of sand or shingle to a beach where the sea has scoured it away. It's a good way to preserve the natural look of a coast, but a big storm can gobble up a beach in a few hours — and it can mean there is more erosion at another part of the coast.

Managed retreat: The plan now for low lying areas is to work with nature not try and fight it.

This means knocking holes in the sea wall to let the sea back in — not everywhere, but in places where the wetlands have room to spread and absorb the rising water. Great news for birds — and good for humans too!

Which way is the sea?

Verdict: Ah, now we're getting somewhere. It's a good idea to work with nature rather than try to fight it, but a solution still needs to be found for coastal towns and cities.

GETTING THE DRIFT

The sea doesn't always attack head on. When the sea flows along the coast it causes longshore drift, pulling sand or shingle with it. Look at Spurn Head or Chesil Beach for some impressive examples. Next time you're on a beach with GROYNES, look at the different levels of beach from one side to the other and work out the direction of drift.

Groynes

FROM SEA TO STREAM

All water is connected. A raindrop falls and collects with others. A tiny stream grows into a bigger stream, joining others to become a river, tumbling over rocks then becoming wider and slower as it reaches the sea. Caring for the oceans really begins with how you look after streams, rivers and lakes.

How do rivers begin? Let's have a look at the longest river in Britain, the River Severn, which is 354km (220miles) long and goes through four counties. This is how a squelchy bit of mountain top turns into a river which is 5 miles wide when it reaches the sea...

1. START WITH A SOGGY BOG

High in the mountains of Wales is a peat bog — partly decomposed plant material, basically waterlogged soil. It soaks up water like a sponge. The water collects into little streams which join up to form bigger streams.

PETE

BOG

Many peat bogs have been drained so the land can be used for grazing or farming — and peat has also been collected as a useful fuel. So the peat bogs that remain need to be looked after.

2. WATER IN A HURRY

Steep mountains mean fast, energetic streams, carving deep grooves into the hillsides and tumbling over waterfalls as they race towards the sea.

3. MEANDERING AROUND...

Smaller rivers join together to make a bigger one, which slows down as it gets to lower ground. As it slows down it cuts into the banks and flows in big loops called meanders.

4. WHAT A BORE!

As its gets nearer the sea and into lower ground, the river slows down even more, especially when it bumps into the incoming tide from the sea which tries to persuade the river to flow backwards. Salt water mixes with the fresh where the two meet.

The tides are so strong at the mouth of the River Severn that sometimes the tide pushes the river backwards in a tidal wave up to 2 metres (6 feet) high for 40km (25 miles). This is called the Severn Bore, and is very popular with surfers and kayakers.

AN EVEN BIGGER BORE! The Qiantang River in China has the world's largest tidal bore. The wave is usually up to 5 metres (6 feet) high, sometimes more, and travels at speeds up to 40kph. The bore is so dangerous that it was not until 2008 that a group of top American surfers persuaded the Chinese Government to let them ride it!

For a lake, being popular can be a bit of a problem. If canoeists, fishermen, walkers, cyclists, waterskiers, sailors, bird watchers, powerboaters and holidaymakers all want to play on the same patch of water, they can get in each other's way. The birds and animals living there, who don't have any say in what goes on, can end up the losers.

LAKES FOR EVERYONE

To keep everyone happy (including the birds and animals) and stop lakes getting spoilt, there are usually rules about how you can use them. This is not to spoil your fun, it's to make sure the area is looked after properly and everyone gets a fair chance to play.

I thought we'd come camping for some peace and quiet...

FAMOUS LAKES — LOCH NESS

Loch Ness is one of the biggest in the UK. It has more water in it than all the other lakes in England and Wales put together, in places it is 230 metres deep (754ft).

It's so deep because it lies along the Great Glen fault, a crack in the earth's crust across Scotland. The Loch Ness monster, of course, doesn't really exist...

I wonder if we'll get a bite today.

FAMOUS LAKES — CONISTON

Coniston Water in the Lake District was made famous when Sir Malcolm Campbell used it to beat the World Water Speed Record. His son Donald carried on the family tradition and in 1966 had a go at beating the 483km/h (300 mph) record in Bluebird K7. He made it to 514km/h (320 mph) but then lost control of the boat which flipped over and sank to the bottom of the lake, taking Campbell with him.

The remains of Bluebird and Donald Campbell were recovered from the lake in 2001. Every year powerboats still come to Coniston from all over the world to take part in Records Week.

That's quackers!

When is a lake not a lake? When it's a reservoir. A reservoir is a lake made by building a dam across a river valley. The valley then floods forming a deep reservoir which collects and stores enough water for us all to use.

FROM MOUNTAIN TO CITY

Where does the water in your tap come from? If you live in Birmingham, it comes all the way from mid Wales. About 360 million litres of water flow down pipes from the Elan Valley reservoirs to the Midlands every day.

Because the lakes are higher than the city, the water travels gently downhill through a very long series of pipes, taking a day and half to make the 117 kilometre (73 mile) journey.

The Elan Valley scheme was built in the late 19th century and consists of five reservoirs with seven dams. Impressive engineering!

Where there's a dam, there's also the possibility of hydro-electric power. Turbines at the base of the dams turn the energy from all that water power into electricity and the five turbines in the Elan Valley dams produce 4.2 megawatts of energy — enough to power more than 5,000 homes.

RUTLAND WATER

The biggest man-made lake in Europe is Rutland Water. In the 1970's the Gwash Valley was flooded to provide water for the growing towns in the area.

After the dam was built, the reservoir took four years to fill and flooded the village of Nether Hambleton. You can still see where the road disappears into the edge of the water!

BACK TO NATURE

Before you jump in for a swim or launch your boat onto a reservoir, check the rules, as many don't allow swimming or watersports. Others, like Rutland Water, specialise in sailing and watery activities, but there are still guidelines to stick to.

Most reservoirs are important nature reserves, and it's only the dam that tells you that they haven't been there forever. Even if you're not allowed to sail on them, they're still great places for walking, fishing, birdwatching and fantastic scenery.

If your old home is one of those at the bottom of the lake, that might not be much comfort!

Centuries ago, there were no roads or railways, just horses and carts on a bumpy track. Rivers were the best way to get around — barges pulled by horses gave a smooth ride that could carry loads of cargo. The problem with rivers, of course, is that they usually wobble all over the countryside — all they care about is finding the quickest route to the sea.

MAN-MADE RIVERS

So if you want to get your boatload of cargo from one town to another, it's a good idea to straighten out bits of river to make the journey quicker. Or even dig yourself a new river altogether, straight to where you want to go. Brilliant! Artificial rivers are called canals and most of them were built in the 19th century to link up all the main industrial towns.

Then railways and roads took over, so canals weren't needed any more. But as roads fill up and oil gets more expensive, perhaps canals as highways will end up being the ecological way to transport goods again!

HOW DO CANALS GO UP HILLS?

Canal engineers were faced with a problem — water can't flow uphill. So they built locks to carry the water up and down hills, like a series of steps.

Locks have a double set of gates to lower and raise the water level without letting it all run away.

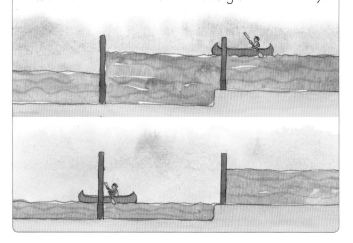

THE END AND THE BEGINNING...

By the middle of the 20th century, the neglected canals began to choke up with weeds and the bridges and locks started to crumble.

Then, just in time, a few people realised that canals would be great fun to go boating on, so they started clearing them out and getting them flowing again.

Now many miles of canals have been cleaned up, the locks fixed, and people who live miles from the sea can get on the water, by canal boat, cruiser, electric boat or kayak.

Wildlife love canals too, so when you go boating, remember that you're visiting our home and treat it with respect.

Another place where man-made waterways have become an important nature reserve is the Norfolk Broads. The Broads are a wide area of interconnecting rivers and lakes in Norfolk, a great place for a boating holiday.

MAN-MADE — BY ACCIDENT!

The Norfolk Broads look so natural that nobody realised that they were man-made until the 1950's.

Norfolk is very low lying and boggy, and if you lived in the area in the 12th century, you'd be struggling to find fuel to burn — there are few trees, no coal and oil hadn't been discovered. So you dug peat out of the bog, dried it out, and burnt that instead.

After a few centuries of peat digging, there were rather a lot of holes in the low lying landscapes which gradually filled with water. Ever practical, the peat diggers used the flooded channels and rivers as useful roads for carrying things around.

Do you think he knows something we don't?

FOR PEAT'S SAKE...
a bit of science...

Peat is compressed organic matter (dead plants, insects, and animals) that has been unable to break down into soil because the land is too boggy. Coal is just peat which has been squashed underground for so long it's turned hard.

Widespread destruction of peat bogs, either through burning or drainage, releases all that locked up carbon dioxide back into the atmosphere. This heats up the earth causing all sorts of problems.

They're important for biodiversity too!

THE BROADS TODAY

The Norfolk Broads are a fantastic place for sailing, motor cruising, walking, fishing, bird watching or just chilling out to admire the view. Like other nature reserves, it's important to enjoy places like this without spoiling them.

Don't forget your binoculars when you go inland. If you're very quiet and very patient, you might be lucky enough to see a few of the creatures who live in and around the waterways. Some are used to humans and don't mind getting close, but others are rare or very shy, so you'll need to keep your eyes open and learn how to stay still and quiet!

SWAN

Everyone recognises the swan, who is bold enough to come tapping on your boat's hull demanding food — but don't feed them and keep your fingers clear of their big beaks!

Did you know that all swans living on open water are owned by the Queen?

MALLARD

Farmyard ducks are related to the popular mallard. The male is the one with the bright colours, while the female is brown. They're very friendly ducks and will often swim up for food — but don't feed them bread!

HERON

You'll spot the heron standing as still as a statue on the riverbank, waiting patiently to catch a fish. It flies with slow beats of its broad wings.

TUFTED DUCK

Easy to recognise by the feathery crest on its head, these common diving ducks can be found on rivers, lakes and reservoirs.

MOORHEN

Similar to coots, but with a red bill and white feathers down its side. Moorhens will make a big noisy fuss if you get too close.

COOT

Coots have a distinctive white bill and black feathers. They usually gather together in groups and can be very noisy!

Why is it a bad idea to feed wild ducks? Moby Duck explains...

It's very tempting to throw us bread — especially when we pester you — but please don't. It's like fast food for ducks and our stomachs aren't designed to handle stodge. Eventually it makes us too ill and slow to forage for the wild food that's good for us.

KINGFISHER

You might only *see* a flash of brilliant *blue* as the kingfisher dives for a fish. Kingfishers are very sensitive to pollution, so their presence along a waterway is a good sign of healthy water.

OSPREY

This impressive fish-eating bird was almost extinct in the 19th century, but if you're lucky you might *see* one on inland waters and estuaries. You won't *see* one in winter, though, as by October they've all flown off to Africa.

MINK

The American mink was first brought to the UK to be farmed for its fur in the early 20th century. Some escaped from the farms and made their homes along the riverbank. They're bold hunters and good swimmers.

OTTER

Don't confuse the mink with the otter, which is much rarer *because* of habitat destruction. Otters are very shy, so you'll have to be very quiet and *still* if you want to spot one. They live in the sea as well as on rivers.

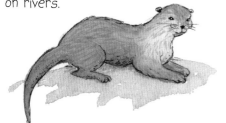

VOLE

This is a rare animal — not helped by the increase of wild mink — vole are their favourite snack. Voles are very shy, and live in burrows on the river bank. They eat nuts, grass and roots and you might *see* one swimming along at the water's edge.

SHREW

Smaller than the vole, the shrew is like a mouse with a long snout. It eats insects and other animals and fish, even managing the occasional frog by using poisonous saliva to kill its prey!

DRAGONFLY

Dragonflies and damselflies look very similar when all you *see* is a flash of colour on the water as they dart around at speeds of up to 48kmh (30mph). Damselflies are usually smaller than dragonflies. If you're lucky and stay very *still*, you may get one to land on your finger!

EMPEROR DRAGONFLY   BLUE DAMSELFLY   RED DAMSELFLY

NEWT

There are several types of newt in Europe, but the great crested newt is the largest and rarest, and is a protected species. You might *be* lucky enough to *see* one on land or around water. Great crested newts grow up to 16cm long.

All sorts of fish live in rivers and lakes, but the Atlantic salmon is a bit special. Not just because it's tasty to eat, but because of the unusual life it leads...

THE LONG JOURNEY

 Baby salmon hatch from eggs laid in the stony bed of a stream high in the hills.

 After a couple of years living in the river, the young salmon head downstream. As they get nearer the sea, their bodies change to be able to live in salt water.

 After swimming around in the North Atlantic Ocean for a few years, feeding in the chilly waters around Greenland, the salmon suddenly get the urge to go home.

 Now here's the clever bit — the salmon find their way back to the exact river they came from and then swim all the way upstream to the place they were born. This is an incredible journey with waterfalls to leap, man-made obstacles and strong currents to swim against all the way.

 The salmon have nothing to eat for the whole journey back upstream. By the time they get home, they're exhausted. After digging a hole in the gravel bed of the stream, the female lays her eggs and many then die of exhaustion. A very few manage to make the journey back down to the sea again where they can feed and grow strong again.

A HELPING HAND

Man-made obstacles can cause a problem for salmon. They may be able to jump up to four metres, but even the cleverest salmon can't leap over a dam.

Fish ladders or fish lifts are built to help the salmon to get past weirs and dams.

NEVER GIVE UP!

Salmon are strong fish, but a waterfall can be a huge obstacle in their journey.

A salmon will spend a whole day trying, if it needs to, until at last it manages to jump high enough.

Next time you're stuck on a problem, take a tip from a salmon — if it's important, don't give up! Not everything in life is meant to be easy.

I knew it was going to be one of those days...

THE SALMON'S SECRET...

Nobody knows how a salmon is able to find its way from the middle of the ocean back to the exact stream it was born. It's one of nature's cleverest secrets.

Right... what's our postcode?

When is a river not a river? When it's a tidal estuary, which usually gets wider as it mixes with salt water and becomes the sea. Many river estuaries have strong tides, as the water is funnelled into a narrower and narrower space. This is both an opportunity and a problem...

HOLDING BACK THE SEA

A storm with strong onshore winds can raise water levels and drive the sea far inland, causing extensive flooding. This is called a storm surge, and there was a really big one in 1953 that caused major flooding along North Sea coasts and rivers.

In one part of the Netherlands, the dyke was all that protected 3 million people from the rising sea. It was holding well, except in one place where it wasn't made of stone. As the water started to break through, the mayor of the town ordered a local skipper to drive his ship into the gap and plug the hole. The ship was called De Twee Gebroeders (The Two Brothers) and it did the trick; the water stopped pouring through and the towns were saved.

THAMES BARRIER

Nearly 2,000 people died in the Netherlands, and 300 in the UK during the 1953 storm. One of the problems was that there was no early warning system for storm surges, and no major flood defences.

To avoid a repeat of the disaster, flood warning systems were put in place and plans were made to protect London from storm surge flooding.

The Thames Barrier took ten years to build and was finished in 1982. It has a set of gates that can be raised to keep extra high tides out. Between 1982 and 2008 it has been used 108 times.

TIDAL ENERGY

A tidal barrage makes energy by trapping the water at high tide and then releasing it through big turbines. The world's first tidal barrage was built in La Rance, France. It's 330 metres long and has been providing clean energy since the 1960's. If a tidal barrage was built across the UK's Severn Estuary, it would be 35 times larger than La Rance. That's a lot of energy — but a big disruption to wildlife and the local environment, so it's not an easy decision to make.

Tidal energy is not a new idea — those smart engineers the Romans caught on to it too — centuries ago, and examples of tide mills are found all over the world. Check out Eling Mill in Hampshire or Woodbridge Tide Mill in Suffolk if you want to see how they work.

The mill pool fills up at high tide, then the sluice gates are shut to hold the water in.

As the water is slowly released, it turns the mill wheel and grinds the flour. Clever!

All inland waters, from the tiniest stream to the biggest lake, do an important job for us and they need to be treated with care and respect. Whether you're in a cruiser, canoe or sailing boat, fishing, walking or cycling, here's a reminder of the part you can play...

Don't 'duck' out of it!

ON THE WATER...

 All your washing up liquid and cleaning fluids go down the sink and into the water, so use phosphate-free products which don't pollute the water.

 When scrubbing the decks, just use water and a brush and scrub hard! Only use cleaning products if you really need to.

 Keep your speed down to avoid disturbing the banks with your wash. Many waterways have speed limits, so make sure you know what they are and stick to them!

 If you're lucky enough to spot nesting birds or wildlife, keep well clear and use binoculars to watch them. If you get too close to baby birds, the mother bird will take fright and abandon them.

 Take care not to pollute the water with engine oil or fuel. Use a spill kit when refuelling outboard engines and keep your bilges as oil-free as you can.

 Make sure no rubbish ends up over the side. Sometimes plastic wrappers can blow away accidentally, so be extra careful.

 Don't throw food waste over the side, thinking that because it's biodegradable it doesn't matter. It still takes a long time to break down and pollutes the water.

CLONK!

WATER WITHIN

Humans are land creatures, unable to fly like us or live in the sea. But you're more connected to the water than you think, and you need the sea as much as we do...

The planet's surface is 70% water, and our bodies are made up of about 70% water.

When you sweat, your sweat is salty. When you cry, so are your tears. Potassium, sodium and calcium make our body salty in about the same proportion as the sea.

WATER, WATER!

After air, water is the most important thing you need to stay alive. You can last without food for quite a long time, but without fresh water only a few days.

Water regulates your temperature and helps your vital organs to work properly. It carries nutrients and oxygen around the body, aids digestion and helps you to get rid of waste.

If your body is short of water, everything gradually stops working. Your brain slows down making you irritable and unable to think clearly. You get headaches and feel as if you've no energy.

Gradually your blood becomes thicker, your heart struggles to pump it round and your vital organs become damaged.

A BIT OF A LOONY?

The moon affects the fluid in your body and brain in the same way it affects the sea — to a very tiny amount, but it can be measured.

The term 'lunatic' comes from the Latin word for moon, because it was thought that people go a bit mad at a full moon.

Yippee! It's a spring tide and I'm a pink pumpkin!

GLUG, GLUG...

We lose over two litres of water a day, through breathing, sweating and going to the toilet. Some is replaced with food, but you still need to drink plenty of water every day (fizzy drinks don't count!)

In hot weather or when playing sport, we lose even more.

GLUG GLUG

But think before buying all those bottles of water — fill a flask from the tap to save cash and waste. If you use bottled water, always recycle the bottles, unless you want to build your own Plastiki!

You can live without many things, but clean water is the most precious. Next time you turn on the tap, say 'thank you', even if your family think you've gone bonkers...

Stop sulking, it was your turn for a bath last month!

ONCE UPON A TIME...

Before the Industrial Revolution there was enough water in rivers and streams to provide families with everything they needed. But gradually cities and towns grew bigger, and we all started to use more water.

Baths and showers, dishwashers, washing machines and flush toilets mean that the average person uses 150 litres of water a day, which is 800% more than your grandmothers would have used.

WATER ON TAP

How does water get into our taps? It's piped from reservoirs then passed through filters to clean it up and take out the fish poo and other rubbish that's found its way into the water.

Then a chemical called chlorine is added to kill off the germs and another chemical called fluoride is added (in some places) to help strengthen your teeth... then it's pumped into big underground pipes called water mains and from there into each building, so that when you turn on the tap clean, drinkable water comes out.

Not everyone has water on tap. If you had to carry all the water you needed like I do, you'd be very careful with it.

DON'T WASTE IT!

You all know it's a bad idea to leave a tap running and waste water, but do you know why? After all, we live on a planet that's covered in the stuff!

It's because only a tiny proportion of that water is fresh and we can't drink the salty stuff. If we use more water than the rain can replace, we're in trouble. Countries with less rain will have serious problems, especially as climate changes make dry countries drier and wet countries wetter.

Water on tap is great, but it's easy to take it for granted and use too much. Flushing the toilet uses a third of all the water that comes into the house. Putting a brick into the cistern saves water as less is used each time you flush.

So now we know how the water gets into our homes — but do you ever give a thought to where it goes when you pull out the plug or flush the toilet?

DOWN THE PLUGHOLE...

All waste water goes into drains that join up and flow down a bigger drain to a sewage treatment plant where the water is filtered and the lumpy bits sieved out. It then has air bubbles pumped through it which encourage helpful micro-organisms to clean it up. Finally it's emptied back into the rivers to begin the journey all over again.

Remember, the amount of water on the planet remains the same. Every bit of water you drink has been recycled many, many times!

CHEMICAL SOUP

The filtering and treatment of waste water can cope with lumps of poo and grime, but it can't filter out all the chemicals that have dissolved into the water.

Washing powders contain phosphates which stay in the water and are washed out to sea.

Persuade your family to buy environmentally friendly washing and cleaning products.

Don't use too many bubbles when you soap and shampoo!

THE GREAT STINK

If you lived in London in the 19th century, all your waste water went straight into the River Thames. And guess where your drinking water came from? That's right, the River Thames. Cholera and other diseases were common.

The summer of 1858 was very hot and dry. Flush toilets had become popular, so the Thames and other rivers were fuller than ever of very smelly sewage. The smell was so nasty that politicians in the Houses of Parliament couldn't work without special perfume-soaked curtains at the windows.

The Great Stink of 1858 led to the design of a proper sewage system for London, still in use today.

DOWN THE DRAIN

Street drains are designed to get rainwater clear of roads and pavements quickly. They carry water straight into rivers and seas without any filtering or cleaning. Often this street water contains pollutants, chemicals, oil or litter from our outdoor activities, so have a care. Don't pour paint or chemical products down the drain — it's not, "out of sight, out of mind".

Oy! Stop that!!

So now we've looked at all sorts of wet stuff, from the deepest ocean to the fluids in your head, what do you think of water now?

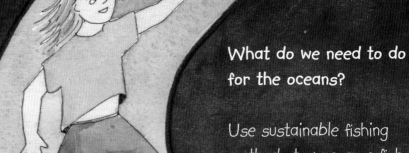

What do the oceans do for us?

Regulate the earth's climate.

Provide the water that keeps us alive.

Keep the land green and growing.

Make a home for more forms of life than you could ever count.

Give us a place to swim, surf, sail and explore.

What do we need to do for the oceans?

Use sustainable fishing methods to preserve fish stocks and avoid by-catch.

Be a lot more careful in how we deal with our plastic waste.

Prevent polluting with oil and chemicals.

Treat animals and birds with care and respect.

Enjoy and appreciate this amazing watery world.

BIG QUESTIONS... WITH BITE-SIZED ANSWERS

WHAT IS A TIDAL WAVE?

A tidal wave is also called a tsunami (pronounce it soo-narmee, which is the Japanese word for harbour wave). It's not caused by tides at all, but by undersea earthquakes or volcanoes. The shock waves ripple out from the centre like a stone thrown into a pond.

Because the ocean is deep, these shock waves are not very *big* out at sea, but they are powerful and fast moving. When they reach the shallower water at the edge of the land they become steeper and higher. By the time they hit land they've become a series of big waves causing damage over a huge area.

Most tsunamis happen around the edges of the Pacific Ocean where there are fault lines in the earth's crust — an active region of volcanoes and earthquakes called the Pacific Ring of Fire.

The edges of the Indian Ocean are also vulnerable. Ten year old Tilly Smith was on holiday in Thailand in December 2004 when she noticed something odd happening on the beach. The water seemed to be bubbling like the froth on a beer! Tilly's geography lesson a few weeks earlier had shown a video of a tsunami — and this was one of the signs. She knew there was no time to lose, persuaded her family she was serious and helped clear the beach of tourists. Minutes later the first wave struck in a tsunami that would kill over 200,000 people, but Tilly's quick thinking (and geography master!) saved at least a hundred lives.

ARE SHARKS DANGEROUS?

Sharks are trouble?

Sharks have a reputation as the scariest fish in the sea. They're big and they're mean with lots of teeth, aren't they? Well, yes and no. They are big and strong and always on the hunt for food, but if they take a nibble at a swimming human it's because they've mistaken them for a fish, seal or turtle. In fact, they don't actually like the taste of humans very much at all, as we're too bony for them, so

they don't usually come back for a second bite! Many surfers have survived some amazingly nasty shark attacks.

The most famous shark is the Great White Shark, over 6 metres long and with a lifespan of up to 100 years.

Sharks are in trouble!

In fact, humans are far more of a threat to sharks than they are to us.

Sharks are hunted for their fins, as shark's fin soup is considered a big treat in some countries. Hundreds are also killed by accident during long-lining. Sharks are starting to go the way of the albatross and becoming dangerously rare. The problem is that we think of sharks as being scary and nasty rather than needing our help. We're more likely to save our support for creatures that are cute or fluffy!

DO SEA MONSTERS EXIST?

There have always been legends about sea monsters big enough to swallow ships, and many stories are based on the giant squid, a monster 18 metres long. Giant squid do exist, but they live deep in the ocean, so they're rarely seen unless a dead one washes up on a beach.

As for other sea monsters, the ocean depths are still largely unexplored, so nobody really knows for sure what lives out there...

WHY IS THE SEA BLUE?

A glass of water is clear and transparent, so why is the sea blue?

The answer lies in sunlight, which scatters as it hits water. Colours with a shorter wavelength, like blue, scatter more easily than those with a longer wavelength, like red.

So red waves go right through water, but blue ones scatter and bounce off the surface of the sea, making it look blue.

IS CORAL A PLANT OR ANIMAL?

Corals may look like plants, but they're actually a combination of tiny plants and animals. The little animals, called polyps, provide a home for the plants (algae) whose by-products provide them with food — so one can't survive without the other. Coral reefs are built up from the limestone skeletons of these animals, and they grow to form an amazing home for thousands of sea creatures, which in turn provide food for larger fish and animals. Coral reefs are the gardens of the sea, and humans love their colour and variety — diving or snorkelling on a coral reef is a never to be forgotten experience.

The biggest reef system in the world is the Great Barrier Reef in Australia. At over 2,600 km long, it can be seen from outer space — not bad for a collection of very tiny creatures! Coral reefs grow all over the world, but they like warm shallow water best with plenty of light.

Corals are in trouble. Humans are damaging these special and delicate places by over-fishing, pollution, dropping anchors on them, stealing bits for souvenirs and, worst of all, messing up the planet's weather so that the sea has to absorb more carbon. This makes the sea more acidic, which kills off the algae, meaning the polyps can't survive. A more acidic sea also dissolves the reefs. Some have disappeared already, so there's another reason to look after the oceans properly and not treat them as our dustbin!

WHY DOES SAVING ENERGY HELP THE PLANET?

The planet has warmed up and cooled down many times in the planet's history as it swings from ice ages to warm periods. The changes normally happen over thousands of years, which means life has a chance to adapt. But human activity is speeding the process up by burning fuel like oil, gas and coal that release carbon into the atmosphere. The carbon forms a layer of insulation round the earth's atmosphere so the heat from the sun can't escape — a bit like being under a duvet.

An overheating planet doesn't necessarily mean nice sunny weather. Small changes in temperature can mess up the complicated pattern of weather systems that we all depend on. Some places will get hotter, some will get colder. Weather will get more extreme, with more storms or more droughts. Low lying countries and coastlines will get flooded out. The delicate balance of life that keeps the oceans healthy will be at risk.

So how do we take some of the heat off and turn global warming back into a gradual natural process that life can adapt to over time? Using clean energy (anything not based on burning fossil fuels) would be ideal, but as few of us have a choice about how our electricity is made, all we can do is try and use less energy wherever possible.

WHAT IS A CARBON FOOTPRINT?

Carbon means carbon dioxide — the gas that's heating up the planet. It's possible to work out how much carbon is used to support your lifestyle. That means everything you need to keep warm, fed, clothed, have fun and travel around. This calculation is called your carbon footprint, and the idea is that we all need to make our carbon footprint as small as possible.

This is easier for people who live simple lives in poor countries, but much harder for those in more developed countries as we depend on so many more energy-guzzling technologies like cars, computers, dishwashers, lighting and heating. New technology is needed to reduce our dependency on carbon based fuels.

WHO OWNS THE OCEANS?

To start with, nobody did. Then in 1702, after years of squabbling about who ruled the waves, an agreement was made that each country owned the sea up to three miles offshore. The three mile limit was decided upon as it was the distance that a cannonball could travel from the shore.

The discovery of oil and gas reserves beneath the sea suddenly made countries want to expand their ownership of the sea. After more wrangling, the limit was extended to 12 miles, with further zones for economic exploitation extending up to 200 nautical miles offshore. Countries also have to look after their waters and take responsibility for their protection. Special agreements were needed where more than one country shared the same patch of sea!

Beyond 200 nautical miles from the coast the sea is called International Waters, or High Seas. This means that it's beyond the laws of any country. Pollution, waste and over fishing don't end at the 200 mile limit, but spread, like the garbage patch, to the whole ocean.

Nobody was interested in the Southern Ocean or Arctic Sea until it looked like there was oil underneath them; now everybody wants a patch! When this happens, governments have to get together and form international agreements to use the seas wisely and fairly.

Eeeek... now I know why it's called the High Seas...

HOW DID THE DEAD SEA GET ITS NAME?

Most oceans have a salinity (salt content) of about 3.5%. But in places where not much fresh water gets into the sea, it can be a lot higher.

The Dead Sea in Israel is an inland sea with not much fresh water flowing into it. It's so salty that it's impossible to sink, and feels a bit like trying to swim in hot treacle!

The Dead Sea is far too salty for anything apart from salt-loving bacteria and algae to live in.

WHAT ARE THE MOST DANGEROUS CREATURES IN THE OCEAN?

What do you think? The Great White Shark? A killer whale? Wrong. From sea snakes to jellyfish, sea urchins, weever fish or even shells, some of the smallest creatures in the sea can be the most deadly:

Here are a few you really don't want to meet:

BLUE-RINGED OCTOPUS

Tiny and pretty, you might see this octopus in a rockpool or washed up on Pacific beaches. But if it feels threatened, the patterns on its skin glow a bright blue and its bite is so poisonous it can cause paralysis and death within minutes.

PORTUGUESE MAN O'WAR

This jellyfish is blown along the sea by its billowing sail, looking a bit like a discarded plastic carrier bag. But if you brush up against its 15 metre long tentacles, they'll give you a painful sting, paralyse your legs or possibly kill you.

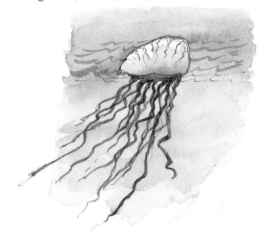

SEA WASP (BOX JELLYFISH)

Probably the most poisonous creature of all is a tiny jellyfish, a transparent blob found in the Indian and Pacific oceans. It looks like an ice cube with tentacles, but its sting is so painful and powerful that it can kill within minutes.

In Australia, far more swimmers suffer from sea wasp stings than shark bites, and some popular beaches have special nets around the swimming areas to keep them safe.

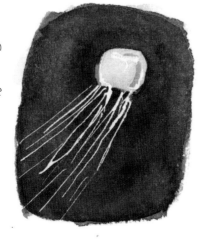

Don't let this put you off going swimming when you're on holiday...

Last one in the sea is a sissy!

WHAT ARE FLOTSAM AND JETSAM?

All good beachcombers need to know what flotsam and jetsam mean. It could be the difference between tidying up the beach and breaking the law!

JETSAM is something that's been thrown overboard from a boat because it's not needed any more, or to lighten a ship in an emergency. If you find jetsam, it's yours to keep. Sadly, these days that usually means rubbish, even though it's against the law to tip rubbish over the side.

FLOTSAM is something that's left floating on the sea or washed up ashore after a shipwreck or having fallen off the deck of a ship. All flotsam is the property of the original owner, not the property of the person who finds it.

This means that if you find something valuable on a beach from a shipwreck or spilt container, you can only take it home if you fill in a form to declare to the Receiver of Wrecks that you've found it. There may be a reward for finding it, or you may be allowed to keep it, but you're breaking the law if you don't declare it.

Um... I'm cleaning up the beach!

WHAT IS A MESSAGE IN A BOTTLE?

Centuries ago the only way sailors could get a message from ship to shore was to put a message in a glass bottle, seal it up and throw it into the sea in the hope that the bottle would float to shore and be found. In battle, it was especially important for the messages to get to the right people, so Queen Elizabeth I appointed an 'Uncorker of Ocean Bottles'. To make extra sure, she made it an offence punishable by death for anyone else to open a bottle washed up on the beach.

More recently, eccentric heiress Daisy Singer Alexander enjoyed writing messages in bottles and dropping them into the Thames. In 1937, three years before she died, she threw a sealed bottle into the river. The note inside expressed her wish to leave half of her entire fortune to the person lucky enough to find the bottle. Twelve years later, the bottle had found its way across the Atlantic, round the top of America, down the Pacific coast and into the hands of a penniless San Francisco dishwasher called Jack as he walked along the beach. As a result of his find, he inherited eight million dollars. Now that's what you call lucky!

HOW CAN YOU SPEND YOUR LIFE ON THE OCEAN?

The ocean is an exciting place and for some people reading about it is not enough. How do you get to be out there, amongst the dolphins, albatross and whales, standing at the bow of a boat, salt spray on your face and the sparkle of flying fish as they skim over the waves?

There are more ways of running away to sea than you might think. Here are just a few suggestions on how to make a career out of the wet stuff:

- Join the navy or merchant navy
- Learn to sail and offer to help people deliver yachts around the world
- Study marine science and get a job on a research ship
- Become a professional diver
- Become a watersports instructor
- Take a job on board a cruise ship

If you just want to get out on the water for fun, there are plenty of choices:

- Learn to sail — the RYA can help you find a good sailing school, or if you live near to a lake or the coast, join your local sailing club. Many of them have junior training sections and it doesn't always cost a lot to join. (There's more information about this at the end of the book)

- Volunteer to help out on a sail training ship — you'll need training first but grants are often available

- Persuade your family to sell your house, buy a small boat and set off round the world (well, it's worth a try!)

Are we nearly there yet?

If you prefer to keep your feet on dry land, there are plenty of ways to appreciate the oceans without getting wet or seasick. The more you learn about something, the more interesting it becomes — so study bird and sea life, find out as much as you can and make each trip to the coast a big adventure!

The bits at the back of the book →

- ## What a load of rubbish!
  Out of sight, out of mind? Look at where it all goes when you throw rubbish 'away'.

- ## What the words mean
  Technical terms explained, from Abyssal to Wingspan

- ## How to find out more
  Useful websites and organisations to help you find out more about the oceans and how to get afloat.

- ## The Go Green team
  The people behind this book who like to make a commotion about the ocean!

- ## The Brains behind the book...

Well, I'm glad we're nearly at the end of the book. All those bad jokes are giving me a haddock!

How long does rubbish take to degrade? Longer than you think!

Most of the rubbish you throw away without a thought will last far longer than you will. Plastic and glass bottles that you use today will still be around at the same time as your great-great-great-great-great-great-great-great-great-great-great grandchildren!

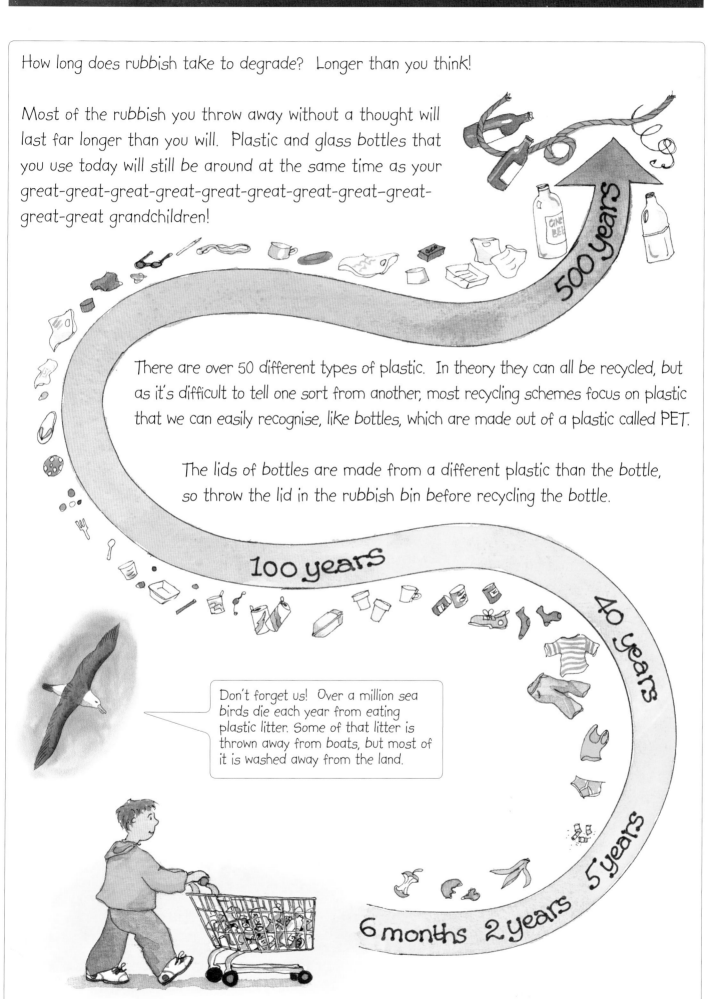

500 years

There are over 50 different types of plastic. In theory they can all be recycled, but as it's difficult to tell one sort from another, most recycling schemes focus on plastic that we can easily recognise, like bottles, which are made out of a plastic called PET.

The lids of bottles are made from a different plastic than the bottle, so throw the lid in the rubbish bin before recycling the bottle.

100 years

40 years

Don't forget us! Over a million sea birds die each year from eating plastic litter. Some of that litter is thrown away from boats, but most of it is washed away from the land.

6 months   2 years   5 years

Rubbish is something we throw away, isn't it? Yes, but have you ever thought about this wonderful place called 'away'? Whether you're on land or sea, have a care. Some ways of throwing things 'away' are better for our earth and oceans than others...

1. REDUCE

Top marks for not filling your house with so much stuff in the first place. And for refusing all that extra packaging at the shops.

Take off as much extra plastic packaging as you can before you go to sea.

3. RECYCLE

You can recycle far more than you think. You know all about paper, tins, plastic bottles, cans and bottles, but did you know you can also recycle mobile phones, paint, toner cartridges and batteries?

If your harbour or marina doesn't already have recycling facilities, ask them to get some!

Oh, and if you're at home, don't forget uncooked food scraps can go in the compost bin.

Smart move!

5. LITTER

Don't even think about it. Ever. Especially now you know where a lot of it ends up.

Stop a minute. Use your head. Where is 'Away'? Just because it's out of your life doesn't mean it's stopped existing.

UCE

USE

YCLE

B SH

2. RE-USE

Your old stuff is somebody else's new stuff. Well done for passing on things you don't need anymore to the charity shop or local freecycle network.

Turn your old gear into cash by doing a car boot sale or have swapping parties with your friends. How about doing a boat jumble at your sailing club to pass on your old sailing gear?

4. RUBBISH!

You've given away, re-used and recycled everything you can, but there's always something left. Nothing for it but the rubbish bin. All your rubbish goes into a big hole in the ground called landfill—not ideal but at least it keeps it out of the oceans.

TER

There is no more "away"...

Abyssal
Abyss means deep, so the abyssal plain is the ocean floor, between the continental shelf and the ridges and even deeper trenches. The abyssal plains cover half the earth's surface but are mostly unexplored. See page 11.

Backwash
The water that flows back into the sea after a breaking wave on a beach. See page 49.

Backwater
A quiet waterway or interconnecting creeks away from the main part of a river, usually busy places for wildlife.

Barrage
An artificial dam or weir across a tidal river. A barrage can be for generating electricity, controlling the flow of the river or preventing flooding. See page 69.

Biodegradable
Anything made of organic material that will break down naturally over time. Compost is a good example of how bacteria can change uncooked food scraps into nourishing soil.

Bioluminescence
Light transmitted by living creatures. It works not by electricity, but by a chemical reaction, and is found in some deep-sea life. See page 11 for examples. See page 11.

Carbon footprint
The total amount of greenhouse gases (carbon dioxide) produced by an individual, a group or country. See page 81.

Cetaceans
Sea mammals that include whales, dolphins and porpoises. See Chapter Three.

Continental shelf
The shallower area of sea extending round the edge of the land, before it dips down to the abyssal plain. During ice ages, much of the continental shelf becomes land.

Coriolis effect
The way the spinning of the earth deflects the wind and water patterns that flow between the equator and the poles. See page 12.

Deposition
The opposite of erosion, deposition is when the sea or river is moving slow enough to dump some of the earth and stones it carries. Fast flowing steep rivers will erode away rock, but slow moving rivers on level ground will drop all the particles, making sand, mud or shingle banks.

Dyke
An artificial wall or earth bank built to protect the land against flooding. The word is also used to mean drainage ditch, so can be a bit confusing!

Ecology

The study of all types of life forms and the way they depend upon each other and the environment.

Endangered

Animals that are in danger of becoming extinct – wiped out completely. Reasons might include over-hunting, or damage to their environment or food supply.

Environment

We're always being told to 'save the environment' - but what is it? The environment is a word that means home. It means our surroundings, the place we all live – planet Earth. It comes from the French word environs meaning surroundings.

Environmentally friendly

Any product or way of life that doesn't damage or pollute the environment.

Erosion

Have a look at deposition. Erosion is the opposite of this - fast flowing rivers or powerful waves can wear away the rock over time and break it into tiny particles.

Estuary

As a river gets nearer the sea the salty water mixes with fresh water and it becomes subject to tides. This tidal section is the estuary. More about rivers in Chapter Five.

Global warming

Too much carbon dioxide in the earth's atmosphere traps the heat from the sun and raises the planet's temperature. More about this on page 81.

Gyre

The large system of ocean currents, largely driven by the Coriolis effect. There are five main gyres – North Pacific, South Pacific, North Atlantic, South Atlantic and Indian Ocean. Find out more about this in Chapter One.

Habitat

The natural environment in which an organism lives – for example, a penguin's habitat is the Antarctic.

Hemisphere

A word that means half a sphere – it also means half a planet. If you chop the earth in two at the equator, it divides into the Northern Hemisphere and the Southern Hemisphere.

Holding tank

A tank connected to a boat's toilet to stop all the waste being pumped out straight into the sea. When it's full, it can either be emptied into special pump-out stations ashore, or let out into the sea if you're well offshore.

Hydro-electric Power generated by fast flowing water, usually by letting water flow past turbines in a reservoir dam.

Hydrologic cycle The natural recycling of water, from sea to vapour to rain to rivers and back to sea again.

Inter-tidal zone The stretch of shoreline between the highest high tide and the lowest low tide.

Krill Tiny shrimps close to the bottom of the ocean food chain that provide food for many fish and animals including blue whales. See page 18.

Maelstrom Another word for a whirlpool, formed by fast flowing tides around steep rocky shores. See page 35.

Migration Some species of birds and animals travel long distances every year in response to seasonal changes, so that they can find a continuous food supply and good place to breed. The Arctic tern travels further than any other migrating bird, flying between Arctic and Southern Ocean waters over the course of a year. That's an impressive 22,000km (13,600 miles).

Ocean Most of the earth's salt water is in the ocean – and although we give them different names, the water in all the oceans is connected. This is called the world ocean or global ocean.

Ocean ridge A range of undersea mountains, like the mid-Atlantic ridge which runs the whole length of the Atlantic Ocean. The ocean ridge usually occurs where two plates of the earth's crust meet. See page 11.

Ocean trench The deepest parts of the earth's crust, forming deep grooves in the ocean floor. Again, trenches often form where one section of the earth's crust is pushed underneath another. See page 11 for a peep into the earth's deepest trench.

Peat Peat bogs are made of partly decomposed organic material. They're dark and squelchy, and a good source of fuel when dried out as, like coal, it has lots of carbon locked up inside it. More about peat and peat bogs in Chapter Five.

Plankton The smallest animals and plants in the sea, but also the most important, because they're at the bottom of the food chain. More about plankton on page 16.

Pollution Damaging the environment, either by chemicals, plastics, oil, heat or light.

Protected A protected environment is a reserve or national park which is carefully managed and looked after to make sure human activity doesn't spoil it. Such places are vitally important for animals and other forms of life that struggle to survive in other places. See page 41.

Ria A deep river estuary, formed when rising sea levels after the ice age flooded a valley.

Salinity The amount of salt in water.

Salt marsh Salt marshes are tidal creeks on low lying river estuaries which partly lie in fresh water but get covered in tidal salty water too.

Sea Can be used to describe all the big blue salty wet stuff with the same meaning as ocean, but a sea is usually a smaller patch of water partly bordered by land, like the North Sea, Mediterranean Sea, Caribbean Sea.

Storm surge If extra strong onshore winds during a storm coincide with low pressure and possibly a high tide, it can lead to coastal and river flooding.

Sustainable Capable of being maintained without running out of resources or causing unrepairable damage. Sustainable fishing means leaving enough fish in the sea to breed so that there's always enough for everyone. Tidal energy is sustainable as it never runs out, like coal or oil will.

Swash The water that runs up the beach and wets your feet if you stand too close to the breaking wave.

Tidal bore A wave, or series of waves, which travels up a river caused by a strong incoming tide. See page 61 for some impressive tidal bores.

Tidal range The difference in height between the lowest tide and the highest tide. Spring tides have a bigger tidal range than neap tides. See page 35.

Tidal stream The movement of water along a coast caused by tides. These currents change hour by hour and can be strong in places.

Trade winds   Regular wind patterns over the oceans, known and used by sailing ships throughout the centuries.

Tsunami   A series of waves caused by an earthquake or volcano. It's also called a tidal wave, although it's nothing to do with tides at all. See page 78.

Turbine   A big cylinder with a propeller in it. Wind or water makes the propeller spin as it flows past and this movement is converted into energy.

Wetlands   Any area of low lying tidal creeks and marshes, like salt marshes.

Wingspan   The size of a bird measured between the tips of its wings.

Inspired to get out on the water but not sure how? Here's some help....

Royal Yachting Association   www.rya.org.uk

The national body for all kinds of watersports, the RYA can offer advice and training on everything from inland waterways to offshore racing. The OnBoard scheme (**www.rya.org.uk/programmes/onboard**) works to give as many young people as possible the opportunity to sail or windsurf.

Ben Ainslie   ## Mike Golding

www.benainslie.com   www.mikegolding.com

Britain's top professional sailors are committed to preserving the marine environment—and not just because they spend most of their time on the water! Ben Ainslie and Mike Golding have both been involved in the making of this book—find out more about their sailing and environmental adventures.

Inspired to find out more about the oceans and how to look after them? Here are a few of the organisations and websites who were most useful in compiling this book:

The Green Blue   www.thegreenblue.org

Meet the Green Blue team on page 97.

Everything you need to know about making sure your watersports don't spoil the water. The Green Blue is the joint environmental programme of the BMF and RYA.

Marine Conservation Society   www.mcsuk.org

Everything you need to know about our seas and beaches and how to protect them. MCS organises beach cleans, monitors sightings of basking sharks, turtles and jellyfish, as well as providing information on how to buy and catch fish wisely **www.fishonline.org**. (**www.goodfishguide.com** to go direct to the Good Fish Guide)

Royal Society for Protection of Birds   www.rspb.org.uk

Everything you need to know about birds, how to recognise them, and even listen to their call. The RSPB also runs the Save the Albatross Campaign—**www.rspb.org.uk/supporting/campaigns/albatross**

Seawatch Foundation   www.seawatchfoundation.org.uk

If you want to find out more about cetaceans (whales, dolphins and porpoises), this site has lots of information, plus a form to fill in to report all your sightings of marine mammals.

Whale and Dolphin Conservation Society   www.wdcs.org.uk

Support the petition to stop whaling, adopt a dolphin and keep up to date with whale and dolphin conservation.

The Seahorse Trust   www.theseahorsetrust.org

Find out more about these delicate and endangered creatures.

Young People's Trust for the Environment   www.ypte.org.uk

Helping young people to understand and get involved in environmental issues. They also run activity holidays for children.

Waterwise   www.waterwise.org.uk

Practical advice and information about how to use water wisely and without waste.

Algalita Marine Research Foundation   www.algalita.org

Founded by Charles Moore who first discovered the Pacific Garbage Patch when he sailed through it, the foundation is dedication to research, education and conservation.

Have a look at **www.ship2shore.blogspot.com** to follow the activities of the research ship 'Alguita'.

www.5gyres.org keeps you up to date with ocean plastic polllution

Plastiki   www.plastiki.com

Follow the adventures of the campaigning catamaran made out of plastic bottles.

Sir Peter Blake Trust   www.sirpeterblaketrust.org

Carrying on the work of the late New Zealand sailor Sir Peter Blake, encouraging young people to care for the environment through adventure and leadership.

Surfers Against Sewage   www.sas.org.uk

Started by a group of surfers who were literally sick of surfing in sewage polluted waters.

Want to know more about how to put the 'Green' back into the 'Blue'? The Green Blue can help...

THE GREEN BLUE TEAM...

"We're a team of people who are passionate about the marine environment. Our job is to help everyone who loves the water to reduce their environmental impact and keep the seas clean and healthy. Here's how we do it..."

RECYCLING AND WASTE MANAGEMENT

"We help boatyards, harbours and marinas to set up recycling schemes, as well as suggesting ways to make sure none of our rubbish ends up in the water!"

EDUCATION

"We want to let everyone know how important it is to look after the marine environment. We find that the more you know and understand, the more care you take.

We've plenty of posters, leaflets, experts and a great website to help spread the word."

SHOPPING

"We'll tell you where you can buy all sorts of good stuff, from wind turbines to non-harmful cleaning products.

It's not just for boats, there's plenty here for everyone."

RESEARCH

"We need to find out as much as we can about the state of the sea and rivers and the impact of our boating activities on wildlife.

So we get together with marine scientists and other experts to get a clear picture about what the problems are and what can be done about them."

Dr Susie Tomson became so fascinated by the sea when on holidays as a child that she decided to become an environmental scientist. Her job is now helping everyone to learn about the sea and use it wisely. She teamed up with some other watery enthusiasts to get the Green Blue going.

Susie and the Green Blue team know that young people are the marine scientists and sailors of the future, and they all thought a children's book about the oceans would be a good idea. They asked Claudia Myatt to draw and write RYA Go Green! as part of the popular RYA Go Sailing! series. Susie gave Claudia some ideas of what to put in the book, and Claudia got her sketch book out to practise drawing fish and albatross.

With thanks also to two of Britain's whizzy sailors, Ben Ainslie and Mike Golding, for their input.

PS Susie says the bad jokes are all Claudia's and nothing to do with her!

Yummy... lunch!

WILDLIFE WATCH

Note down any marine wildlife that you recognise —
and draw a sketch of it too if you can

Now it's your tern to
write things down...

WILDLIFE WATCH

Note down any marine wildlife that you recognise —
and draw a sketch of it too if you can

Now it's your tern to
write things down...

Where there's water, there's life